The Brethren

JOHN GRISHAM

Level 5

Retold by Nancy Taylor
Series Editors: Andy Hopkins and Jocelyn Potter

Library Learning Information

Idea Store® Bow
1 Gladstone Place
Roman Road
London E3 5ES

020 7364 4332

Created and managed by
Tower Hamlets Council

Pearson Education Limited
Edinburgh Gate, Harlow,
Essex CM20 2JE, England
and Associated Companies throughout the world.

ISBN 0 582 45352 6

First published in the UK by Century 2000
This edition first published 2001

Typeset by Ferdinand Pageworks, London
Set in 11/13pt Bembo
Printed in Spain by Mateu Cromo, S. A. Pinto (Madrid)

Published by Pearson Education Limited in association with
Penguin Books Ltd, both companies being subsidiaries of Pearson Plc

For a complete list of the titles available in the Penguin Readers series please write to your local
Pearson Education office or to: Marketing Department, Penguin Longman Publishing,
5 Bentinck Street, London W1M 5RN.

Contents

Introduction

Follow the money, and you'll find your winner . . .

Trumble Federal Prison is temporary home to a group of non-violent criminals, including lawyers, bankers, drug dealers, and three former judges who call themselves the Brethren. The judges run a small law practice with the other prisoners as their clients, but they spend most of their time organizing an illegal pen-pal scam.

Things are going smoothly, and money is pouring in, until the scam catches the wrong pen pal, a powerful man with dangerous friends. Suddenly, the Brethren's quiet days are over.

Judges, prison, and politics . . . Grisham's eleventh bestselling novel may sound serious, but Grisham says that the book is probably the funniest he has written.

John Grisham was born on February 8, 1955 in Jonesboro, Arkansas. He dreamed of becoming a professional baseball player, but realized that he did not have the talent for this and changed his goals. He graduated from law school in 1981 and practiced law for almost ten years.

But even as a hard-working lawyer, Grisham found time for his hobby: writing novels. *A Time to Kill* (1988) took three years to write and was not a success at the time, but Grisham finished *The Firm* in 1991. He sold the movie rights for this novel for $600,000, and suddenly everyone wanted to read his books.

Since then, Grisham has become known as the master of the legal adventure novel, and today millions of readers eagerly look forward to each new Grisham book. His books have appeared in twenty-nine languages. Six of the novels have been made into movies. All of them are Penguin Readers.

Chapter 1   The Brethren at Work

The judges entered the room.

"All rise. The Lesser Court of North Florida is now ready for business," announced T. Karl, the former owner of several banks in Boston. His voice was loud and serious, but no one stood up as the judges walked to their seats. This wasn't a real courtroom. It was the cafeteria of Trumble Federal Prison, and the three judges, plus most of the men in the room, were criminals with a prison sentence.

However, everyone at Trumble took the weekly business of this court very seriously. First of all, although the judges wore old shiny green robes from a local church, and one of them didn't wear shoes or any clothes under his robe, all three men had been real judges in their previous lives. And, secondly, everyone— prisoners, guards, and even prison officials—accepted the decisions of the three judges: Joe Roy Spicer, Finn Yarber, and Hatlee Beech, better known as "The Brethren." These three formerly important men heard complaints, settled arguments, and generally made Trumble a more peaceful place to live. Their decisions were as quick and fair as they could make them.

Spicer had dealt with small cases for years and could recognize a liar at fifteen meters. Beech and Yarber had spent their careers in courtrooms and had no patience for long arguments and technical discussions. The three of them kept things moving and, in general, gave satisfaction; as the Brethren, they'd regained a certain level of importance and respect, even as prisoners.

The judge dressed only in his church robe was the Honorable* Finn Yarber, a sixty-year-old from California. He'd been sent to Trumble for seven years for not paying his income taxes. But Yarber explained, to anyone who'd listen, that the real

---

* The Honorable: a title of respect for judges and other government officials.

reason for his prison sentence was his enemy: a new governor who hated forward-thinking judges like Finn Yarber.

As a judge Yarber hadn't liked to send people to prison, and he'd never sent anyone to the electric chair. But times had changed and people wanted criminals to be put in jail for a long time. They wanted blood, and the new governor promised them that they'd get it. He called for a revote on Judge Yarber and threw him out of office. Then, in an unexpectedly nasty move, he advised the tax department to look into Yarber's recent tax payments; soon the former judge was serving time at a federal prison in Florida.

Finn Yarber had been at Trumble for two years already but was still struggling with his bitterness. He believed that he was innocent and planned to defeat his old enemy one day. He spent a lot of time outside, walking, baking in the sun, and dreaming of another life.

Sitting to Yarber's left was Joe Roy Spicer. Short and round, he was a Justice of the Peace,* rather than a real judge. He hadn't had any legal training; he hadn't even graduated from high school. But because he'd worked in his father's country store for twenty years, everyone in Joe Roy's little corner of Mississippi knew him and elected him to his position. Joe Roy had enjoyed his small role in local politics, but unfortunately, he was greedy and was caught selling local government contracts. He understood people, especially their weaknesses; his two partners could deal with legal theory.

The third member of the Brethren, Hatlee Beech, had fallen from the greatest height. He was fifty-six years old, the youngest of the three, and facing nine more years in Trumble. He worried about his health and was sure that he was going to die in prison. Beech had been a traditional federal judge in East Texas, a man who liked to decorate his speeches with passages from the Bible. He'd had political ambitions, a nice family, and a very wealthy

---

* Justice of the Peace: a low-level judge with limited powers.

wife. He'd also had a drinking problem which was a secret until he hit and killed two young walkers in a state park. The car Beech had been driving was owned by an attractive young lady who he'd met in a bar that evening. She was found in the front seat of the car with no clothes on, too drunk to walk. Her drunken "friend," Judge Hatlee Beech, was sent to prison for twelve years.

Back in court, T. Karl stood behind his cafeteria table and announced the case of the day to the audience and to the three judges: "Picasso against Sherlock."

"What's the charge, T. Karl?" asked Judge Spicer.

"Sherlock has been urinating on Picasso's roses. He wants this stopped and he wants $500 to repair the damage."

A little outdoor urination was not something to worry about at Trumble, but $500 was a serious matter.

The pale pink roses were called Belinda's Dream. Picasso had spent three years writing letters to Washington to get permission for his hobby from the federal government. As soon as he had it, the rose bed became his life. He could be seen early and late in his little garden next to the gym. His roses—the beautiful Belindas—were watered and fed and even talked to with loving care.

But then Sherlock began urinating on the pale pink roses just for fun. He wasn't fond of Picasso anyway, because the fat little gardener was a famous liar, and "watering" a liar's roses seemed a good idea to Sherlock.

The pale pink Belindas began to turn a dull yellow, and Picasso began to worry. He didn't know what was happening until he caught Sherlock in the act. Picasso screamed and threatened, but Sherlock just laughed and walked away. That was when Picasso took his case to the Brethren.

For three hours the judges listened to two fat middle-aged men argue about who had urinated where, and how often. Joe Roy Spicer passed the time by deciding which college basketball games to bet on and by thinking about the past.

3

Joe Roy had made almost $300,000 from selling contracts, but the federal lawmen only knew about $100,000. Another $90,000 was hidden in his backyard in Mississippi; he and his wife had spent the rest on the good life. They'd bought expensive cars and had flown to Las Vegas, first class.

Now his dream was to return to Las Vegas as a professional gambler. He'd lost plenty of money on card games, but he was still sure that he could win in any gambling house in the world. He'd go home one day, dig up his $90,000, and move to Vegas, with or without his wife.

She used to come to Trumble every three weeks, but now she hadn't been in four months. Maybe she was busy spending his money with a new boyfriend. The idea drove Joe Roy crazy—not the idea of a boyfriend, but the idea that she'd found his hidden money. He wanted to rescue his $90,000 and go to Vegas. One day he'd be living the high life again. With or without his wife.

Hatlee Beech interrupted Joe Roy's daydream. "I've heard enough. I think we're ready to make our decision."

The Brethren whispered together for a few minutes, scratching their heads and listening to each other's comments. Then each of the judges wrote something on a piece of paper.

Judge Yarber stood up and said, "By a vote of two to one, we have reached a decision. It is now forbidden to urinate on the roses. Anyone caught doing so will pay $50. Picasso receives nothing for the damage to his roses."

The three judges were in agreement, but they always announced a two-to-one decision. This gave each of them a bit of protection if there were any arguments outside of the court.

"That's all for today," T. Karl reported. "Court will meet next week. Same time. Same place. All rise."

"I want money for my damaged roses," shouted Picasso, the wronged gardener. "I demand justice!"

"So do I," laughed Sherlock. "I'm not paying to urinate."

"A good decision," Yarber said as he left. "Both sides are unhappy."

The prison guard at the back of the room laughed. The Brethren's weekly court was the best show at Trumble.

Chapter 2   The Candidate

Aaron Lake had served in Congress★ for fourteen years, but he still drove his own car around Washington, D.C. He didn't want a driver or a bodyguard—he preferred to have a little time alone, away from his crowded office and all the people demanding his time and attention. He enjoyed being alone. It gave him time to listen to his favorite guitar music and to think about his responsibilities to the people of Arizona, the people who had put him in Congress.

Lake was single, a widower, with a small stylish house in the fashionable part of Georgetown and a grown-up daughter who was a schoolteacher in Santa Fe, New Mexico. His parents were dead. His wife of twenty-nine years had died three years before.

He followed the highway to Langley and the offices of the CIA† for a meeting with Teddy Maynard, the CIA director and, in many people's opinion, the most powerful man in the country. Maynard rarely left Langley. He was in a wheelchair and in constant pain, so he called congressmen to him. This was Aaron Lake's first meeting at Langley. He was nervous and excited; something important was in the air.

As Lake was being led toward his large, square, windowless office, the director sat alone looking at a big screen on which the face of the congressman was frozen. It was a recent photo, taken at a Washington party where Lake had half a glass of wine, ate baked chicken, no cake, drove himself home, alone, and went to bed before eleven o'clock.

★ Congress: the national law-making body of the United States.
† CIA: the Central Intelligence Agency; the United States government department responsible for collecting information about foreign goverr

Lake was attractive—naturally light red hair with almost no gray, dark blue eyes, square chin, really nice teeth. He was fifty-three years old and looked great. He exercised 30 minutes a day on a rowing machine, was 182 centimeters tall and weighed 72 kilograms. Lake's regular date for official events was a wealthy widow from Bethesda. The CIA hadn't found a single bad habit.

Lake had never aimed at higher office—he enjoyed Washington and the life of a congressman too much. He loved the city: the crowds, good restaurants, small bookstores, coffee bars. He liked theater and music, and he and his wife had never missed an event at the Kennedy Center for the Arts.

In Congress, Lake was known as someone who spoke well, was intelligent, honest, and loyal, and worked hard for his Arizona district. Because it was the home of four large weapons and army vehicle contractors, Lake had become an expert on America's military strength.

Teddy Maynard had been through a lot in his fifty years with the CIA. He'd had more adventures than a hundred congressmen, but looking at the innocent face of Aaron Lake he felt a new excitement. The CIA was planning to do something that had never been done before.

They'd started with a hundred politicians. They'd looked at each man's life very carefully, and now there was only one: Aaron Lake. The screen went black as Teddy Maynard turned in his wheelchair and prepared to meet his candidate.

After the formal greetings, Aaron Lake and Teddy Maynard sat opposite each other at a long table. Teddy pushed a button and another face appeared on the large screen.

"Do you recognize him?" Teddy asked.

"Natli Chenkov," the congressman answered proudly. He kept himself informed about Russian politics. "Also known as Natty."

"That's him. Close connections with the military, very ambitious, brilliant mind, and right now the most dangerous man in the world," Teddy explained.

A new picture appeared on the screen.

"This is a map of an area north of Moscow. Chenkov is building up an enormous store of weapons in this region."

"Where's the money coming from?" asked Lake.

"From oil, drugs, anything that Chenkov can sell. He knows how to do business," said Teddy with admiration.

"But what's the purpose of all of this military equipment?" asked Lake.

"Russia is falling apart. Their new system is a joke. Workers aren't getting paid. Children and old people are dying because there are no medicines. Ten percent of the population is living on the streets. Twenty percent is hungry. The time is perfect for a new leader who'll promise to save the country, and Mr. Chenkov has decided that he'll be the new leader."

"What about the army?" asked the congressman.

"He has the army with him. The people will follow him because things are so bad. He'll take over the country and dare the United States to stop him. We'll be the bad guys again," explained Teddy. "And it won't stop with Russia. He'll need cash, and he'll look for it by taking over the weak countries around him. If we don't take action, Chenkov'll be the most famous man in the world a year from now."

"Do you think that he'd risk a Third World War?"

"I can't answer that," said Teddy, "but he's putting people in place, he's getting things ready."

There was a long pause as the two men thought about the end of the world. Teddy also thought about Lake. He liked him a lot. They'd made the right choice. He was the perfect candidate.

After coffee was brought in and Teddy took a telephone call from the White House, the meeting with Aaron Lake continued.

"I think you know that our military isn't prepared for a war with the Russians," Teddy began again.

"We're at 70 percent," Lake said confidently.

"At 70 percent, we'll get a war we cannot win. Chenkov is spending every dime on military equipment. At the same time, we're cutting our military spending. Chenkov is going to have two million hungry soldiers who are anxious to fight and to die if necessary."

"Can't you stop Chenkov now?" the congressman asked.

"Absolutely not. It's too early. We don't want him to know that we know. It's the spy game, Mr. Lake."

"So what's your plan?" Lake asked. He knew he shouldn't be so bold. There was probably a line of congressmen waiting outside for their few minutes with the CIA director.

But Teddy was in no hurry to finish his meeting with Aaron Lake. In fact, he was anxious to share his plans with him.

"The first stage in the presidential election is in New Hampshire in two weeks. Not one of the seven candidates is talking about increasing military spending. They don't understand what's going on in the world." Teddy paused and tried to move his useless legs to a more comfortable position. "We need someone new, Mr. Lake, and we think it's you."

"You can't be serious!" said Lake.

"You know I'm serious, Mr. Lake," Teddy said steadily, and there was no doubt that Aaron Lake had walked into the director's well-planned trap.

"All right, I'm listening," said Lake, after he took a few seconds to get his breath.

"It's very simple. You wait until after the New Hampshire contest and then surprise everyone by announcing that you're a candidate. You'll have only one thing to say—that the American military is weak and that you will double our defense spending in your four years as president."

"Double it? Is that necessary?"

"It's necessary if we're facing a war, Mr. Lake. We're low on everything—soldiers, weapons, airplanes, ships. If we continue to reduce the amount we spend on defense, we're dead."

"But where will the money come from?"

"Mr. Lake, don't worry about the money. We're going to frighten every man, woman, and child in this country. At first, they'll think you're a crazy nobody from Arizona who wants to bomb the world. But then we'll create a few dangerous situations on the other side of the world. Americans will begin to feel threatened, and suddenly you'll sound like the smartest man in American politics. Nobody will object to tax money paying for a stronger America."

A thousand questions raced through Aaron Lake's mind, but he only asked the most important one, "But how will I pay for a presidential campaign? I don't have that kind of money."

"Campaign money won't be a problem either, Mr. Lake. The industries which make military equipment will be very happy to hear your plans for defense spending. You make the speeches, do the advertisements, run the campaign. The money will pour in— I guarantee it."

"I'm single. There's only been one unmarried president," said Lake thoughtfully.

"You're a widower, the husband of a very beautiful, intelligent lady who was respected in Washington and back home. You had a good marriage. You're a solid candidate. If we couldn't find anything wrong with you, no one else'll be able to either.

"Sleep on it, Mr. Lake. A man should have twenty-four hours before making such a decision," said Teddy.

"That's a wonderful idea. I'll have an answer tomorrow."

"And, Mr. Lake, no one knows we've had this little chat," warned Teddy.

"Of course not," agreed Aaron Lake.

Chapter 3   The Scam

Trumble Federal Prison was a good place to be if you had to be in prison. It was officially referred to as a camp, and only non-violent prisoners were sent there. It had no fences, no guards with guns or mean attitudes, no watchtowers. A prisoner could simply walk away from Trumble if he chose to, but few did.

Each man had an easy job which he did for very low pay.

They also had comfortable rooms, a clean cafeteria with good food, a gym, a game room, several TV rooms, a library, a church, a hospital, and unlimited visiting hours.

The big, modern library was especially important to the Brethren. It had the latest office equipment and lots of law books which no one used without the Brethren's permission.

On a typical day, the Brethren spent between six and eight hours in the library. Other prisoners met with the three judges by arrangement and received expert advice on their legal situations. Hatlee Beech and Finn Yarber helped them to reduce their time in prison and advised them on marriage and financial problems. The Brethren were paid for their legal work, although there were rules against this. Often families outside paid the charges to the judges' lawyer in Neptune Beach, Florida. This lawyer, Trevor Carson, then took his 30 percent and put the rest of the money in the Brethren's bank account in the Bahamas.

But the money they received for legal advice was nothing compared to the money they planned to make from their pen-pal scam. When they were working on this, the three men locked themselves in the conference room in the library.

Spicer met with Trevor the day after the Picasso case and returned to the library with some really good mail. He closed the office door and waved an envelope for Beech and Yarber to see.

"Look at this. It's for Ricky," Spicer told his two partners.

"Who's it from?" Yarber asked.

"Curtis in Dallas. The guy who owns jewelry stores. Listen." Spicer smiled and began to read: "*Dear Ricky: Your last letter made me cry. I read it three times before I put it down. You poor boy. Why are they keeping you there in that awful place?*"

"Where does Curtis think Ricky is?" asked Yarber.

"Ricky's in an expensive center for rich kids with drug problems," explained Spicer. One of his jobs was to remember what story they'd sent to each of Ricky's pen pals. "Ricky's very rich, cruel uncle is paying. The poor boy's been in for a year and has been very good. No drugs for all that time. But the rich uncle wants him locked away and won't send him any money to spend on his personal needs. May I continue now?"

"Please do."

"Curtis writes: *'Your uncle is evil. I know—my father was very rich, but he never had time for me. I'm sending you a check for $1,000 so you can buy a few things for yourself.*

"'*Ricky, I can't wait to see you in April. I've already told my wife that I'm going to an international diamond show in Orlando on April 10. She has no interest in going with me.'*"

"How old is this guy?" asked Beech.

"He's fifty-eight, three adult children, two grandchildren. Listen: *'We have to meet in Orlando. Are you sure you'll have your freedom in April? I look at your photograph every hour. Your eyes tell me that we should be together.'* The rest is more sweet talk, but here's the check," finished Spicer.

"When do we send our demand for the big money?" Yarber asked.

"Let's exchange one or two more letters. After we have a couple more love letters from Curtis to Ricky, we'll drop the bomb on him. He'll send us a nice fat check to protect his good name."

They worked on the story—more pain, more problems for the sweet young boy. They'd taken Ricky's photograph from the cabinet of another prisoner. Their lawyer had copied it, and they'd sent it to more than a dozen lonely men across America. It was a photograph of a handsome, healthy young man at college, smiling at the camera as he stood on a tennis court in the sun.

Beech and Yarber wrote Ricky's letters. Each of their lonely pen pals had made the mistake of answering the simple advertisement that Trevor had placed in the back of a gay magazine:

Single, white male in 20s looking for kind and discreet gentleman in 40s or 50s to exchange letters with.

This one little advertisement had brought in sixty letters. Spicer

11

read each one and decided who would get a letter and a photograph from Ricky. Spicer wasn't any good at writing, but the idea for the scam had come from him. He knew about some criminals in a Mississippi prison who had made more than $700,000 from a similar business. Spicer also met with Trevor, who brought the mail.

"Gentlemen," said Joe Roy, "this one is from Quince."

Quince was a rich banker in a small town in Iowa. He'd written six letters to Ricky and had even sent a photograph of himself. It showed a white 51-year-old man with thin arms and legs, a fat little stomach, and not very much hair—his wife and three children at his side.

Spicer began to read: "'*Dear Ricky: I did it! I used a pay phone and sent a money order to the company in New York that you suggested. They were very helpful and very discreet. I was so nervous, but I've reserved an apartment ($1,000 a night!) for a week at a gay vacation village. I never dreamed of a trip to the Caribbean! I'm so proud of myself.*

"'*And I have a wonderful idea. Let's go to our apartment, lock the door, and stay there. Seven days and nights together!*'"

Spicer smiled and shook his head in disgust.

He continued: "'*I'm so excited about our little trip. I've finally decided to discover who I really am, and it's because you've given me hope and have made me brave. Ricky, I can never thank you enough.*

"'*Please write back immediately. Our flight is on March 10—tell me if that's OK. Take care, my Ricky. Love, Quince.*'"

"I feel sick," Spicer said, but he was ready to start work. There was a lot to do.

"Let's pull him in now," Beech said.

The others quickly agreed.

"How much?" Yarber asked.

"At least $100,000," said Spicer. "His family has owned banks for more than a hundred years. His father's still running the business and is the most important man in their hometown. He'd go crazy if anyone found out that his son was in love with

Ricky." Men like Quince wouldn't go to the police and complain of blackmail. They had too much to lose.

Before long, Beech and Yarber had a letter to send to Quince. Yarber read it aloud: "'*Dear Quince: So nice to get your letter of January 14. I'm so happy that the gay vacation has been arranged. There's only one problem, though. I won't be able to go to the Caribbean with you. First, I'm in a prison, not in an expensive drug center. And, I'm not gay. I have a wife and two kids, and right now they're having a hard time paying the bills. But you can help, Quince. I need some of your money. I want $100,000. You send it, and I'll forget the Ricky business and the gay vacation and no one in Bakers, Iowa, will ever know anything about it. If you don't send the money, I'll send copies of your letters to the newspaper in Bakers.*

"'*It's called blackmail, Quince, and you're caught. It's mean and criminal, and I don't care. I need money, and you have it.*'"

"It's beautiful," said Spicer. He could see himself in Las Vegas already, gambling with his share of the money.

The Brethren left their office and went to their separate rooms. They didn't think about what would happen if they were caught. Instead, they dreamed of what they'd do with the money. This would be the first of many big paydays. The letters were coming in, the scam was working nicely. The three judges planned to get very rich.

Chapter 4   Who in the World is Aaron Lake?

Teddy Maynard was seated at his big table, talking to James York, his personal assistant.

York said, "Lake was on the phone until three this morning, talking to friends in Arizona. They were surprised that he wants to be president."

"Was he discreet? Did he keep our secrets?"

"He certainly did."

Teddy took another pill from one of the many bottles on the

table. "York, tell me that we're not missing anything about Lake. Is he really clean? No surprises from his past?"

"Chief, we've looked at everything for six months. There's nothing in his background that can hurt us."

"No problems with alcohol, drugs, women, gambling?"

"No, sir. He's clean, straight, smart—a nice guy. Really wonderful," said York.

By eleven o'clock that morning, Aaron Lake was sitting in Teddy Maynard's office again.

"Well, Mr. Lake, are you ready to accept our deal?"

"Deal? I didn't know it was exactly a deal," said Lake.

"Oh, yes, Mr. Lake, it's a deal. We promise to get you elected, and you promise to double defense spending and get ready for the Russians," explained Teddy.

"Then you have a deal."

"That's good, Mr. Lake. I'm very pleased. You'll make an excellent candidate and a fine president."

It all seemed too easy to Lake. President Aaron Lake. He couldn't believe it. He'd have a place in history.

James York came into the office and the three men settled down to plan the campaign. They decided when Lake would announce that he was a candidate; they found a campaign manager; they designed the first TV advertisements.

"Can we pay for all of this?" asked Aaron Lake.

"Mr. Lake, money won't be a problem. We can buy everything that's important," said Teddy.

"But the message is important, too, isn't it?" asked Lake a bit nervously.

"Oh, it is. Our message is life and death. Our message will change the world and protect our country."

After Aaron Lake left his office, Teddy thought about the campaign. He was certain that Mr. Aaron Lake would win the election and become the next President of the United States.

◆

Trevor Carson had a very small law office in Neptune Beach near Jacksonville, Florida. He'd been in this cheap, dusty office for twelve years. In the first few years, he spent several hours every day staring in wonder at the gentle waves of the Atlantic Ocean. He'd grown up in the middle of America, far away from any ocean. But these days, he spent all of his free time in Pete's Bar and Grill, his favorite place to get pleasantly drunk at lunchtime and in the evenings.

Very few clients visited Trevor's office because he was afraid of courtrooms and judges. This meant that he only worked on the most boring cases, like housing contracts and insurance claims, and it also meant that he made very little money.

Joe Roy Spicer had heard of Trevor through one of the Brethren's Trumble clients, and now Trevor was the judges' partner on the outside. In addition to carrying mail in and out of the prison and running the Brethren's bank account, Trevor also found out important information about Ricky's pen pals. Of course, the unambitious lawyer would go to prison if the pen-pal scam was ever discovered, but for the promise of easy money and staying out of court, he was ready to gamble with the Brethren.

No lawyer in history had visited Trumble prison as often as Trevor. He knew all the guards by name, signed the visitors' book, showed his driver's license, and opened his bag for inspection on each visit. The only thing he carried in his bag was an envelope marked "Legal Papers," which were allowed in the visitors' room. As he stepped into the room, he very quickly removed two twenty-dollar bills from his pocket. If he handed this money to the guard just inside the door, the prison camera didn't see them. This guaranteed that the guard didn't watch or listen to their meeting.

On this particular morning, Joe Roy handed over the check from Curtis, and said, "Here's $1,000 to put in the bank."

"Great," said Trevor. "Anything else?"

"We're ready to demand money from the banker," Joe Roy said, giving Trevor a pale blue envelope addressed to Quince Garbe.

"How much are we asking for?"

"A hundred thousand," said Joe Roy quietly.

"Will he pay it?" Trevor asked, trying not to sound too excited.

"He's got it, and he'll pay. He can't risk having his secrets discovered. Tell our bank that the money is coming."

"Right. As soon as I get back to the office."

In twenty-three years as a lawyer, Trevor had never earned $33,000—his share of the Quince money—in a year. Suddenly, he could see it, touch it, and, though he tried not to, he began spending it—$33,000 for doing nothing except carry letters and make phone calls.

He tried to stay calm. "Do you want me to put any money on the Kentucky–Arkansas basketball game tonight for you?" he asked Joe Roy, the professional gambler.

"I'll put a hundred on Arkansas," said Joe Roy.

"I think I will, too," said Trevor. It felt great to have some money. He could pay his bill at Pete's Bar and his credit card debts, and he could enjoy placing some bets.

Things were definitely improving.

♦

The music played, the audience cheered, the TV cameras watched, as Aaron Lake walked onto the stage at the Trilling helicopter factory. He was there to announce that he was a candidate for President of the United States. Three days earlier no one had heard of Aaron Lake, but now he was these people's hero.

"My name is Aaron Lake, and I'm going to be the next president." More shouting and cheering, more music. Teddy Maynard had planned every detail. Aaron Lake's speech covered three areas: an attack on the present government for reducing spending on defense; a warning about foreign governments which threatened America's safety, and a plan for dealing with both of these problems: to double spending on defense during his four years in office.

When Lake finished, the crowd went wild. The 4,000 Trilling employees built military helicopters, and with this man in the White House they could imagine a very bright future.

At Langley, Teddy Maynard and York watched and were satisfied with Aaron Lake's performance.

"He's very good," York said quietly.

"Yes, we chose the right man."

◆

Sitting alone in one of several TV rooms at Trumble, Hatlee Beech watched the same news program. He was probably the only man in the prison who was interested in what was going on in American politics. He was surprised that he'd never heard of Aaron Lake. Probably just one of the crazy candidates that always appeared during a presidential election.

After the news report on Lake, Hatlee Beech sat through a few more stupid shows and thought about his past.

Three years, one month, one week. Beech counted the days he'd been in Trumble, rather than the days that were left. Just four years ago he'd been a respected federal judge. His wife was an unpleasant woman, but they had three fine kids in college, a large share of her family's oil fortune, and plenty of important friends. They planned to grow old together—where else was there to go?

Certainly not to prison.

But prison was where Hatlee ended up because of his drinking. He didn't remember very much about the beginning of the evening, when he met the young woman at the bar. He wasn't interested in sex with her, but it was nice to have an attractive woman to drink with. He didn't remember anything about the car ride or about the two young people on the road. He only remembered waking up in jail and then losing everything: his wife, his children, his friends, his career, his money. He had nothing left except nine more years in prison. He'd be sixty-five when his time was finished, but he was sure he'd be dead before then. They'd carry him out of Trumble in a box.

Suddenly, his attention was caught by a political advertisement. He heard a serious voice claiming that the American way of life would end if military spending wasn't increased fast. Then black-and-white pictures of foreigners with guns ready for battle, burning buildings, crying women and children. It was very well done, ran for a minute and a half, cost a lot of money, and delivered a message no one wanted to hear. No smiles, no warmth. Just the serious voice: "Lake Before It's Too Late."

Not bad, thought Beech, but who in the world is Aaron Lake?

◆

For Quince Garbe, February 3 would be the worst day of his life.

It began pleasantly enough with a late breakfast, and then his usual drive to work in his old, but expensive car. Quince was an important man in Bakers, Iowa, a member of the Garbe family and the only son of the 81-year-old president of the bank. Quince parked in his reserved space behind the bank and made a quick trip to the post office. For years he'd had a private box there, away from his wife and especially away from his secretary.

Quince was tired. Tired of taking orders from his father, tired of the bank, tired of his wife, tired of Iowa and snow. More than anything, he wanted to be in the Caribbean with Ricky. That morning in February he just wanted a note from Ricky saying that he was excited about the trip, too.

There were three letters waiting for him. He quickly picked them up and hurried to his office. He rushed past his secretary and locked his office door behind him. He'd seen that one of the letters was from his dear Ricky. He sat on the sofa and put on his reading glasses, breathing heavily because he was so excited.

The words hit him like bullets. He made a strange, painful sound: shock, disbelief. He threw the letter on the floor and walked around his office, ignoring the cheerful faces of his wife and children in the photographs on his desk. The letter was a joke, he told himself. But he knew it was a professional scam.

18

All of his life he'd fought his desires, but then one day he'd opened the closet door a little. He'd dreamed that he could leave Bakers and escape to the beach, where he could have fun with a handsome young friend and maybe never come home again. Stupid, stupid, stupid.

He thought about killing himself, but he really didn't want to die. Maybe he should go to Florida and find "Ricky" and tell the police about him, but he knew he couldn't do that.

His father was an old man, but he still ruled the bank and had control of all the money. When he died, Quince and his sister would share $10 million, but if his father found out about "Ricky," he'd get nothing. He'd have to find the money and buy his way out of this mess. He knew a couple of less-than-honest property dealers. He could help them with a few questionable deals. They'd know how to raise the cash.

◆

DEFENSEPACKAGE, or D-PAC, as it became known very quickly, entered the mysterious world of political finance with more money and more power than any similar group in recent history. The organization existed to raise cash and support for Aaron Lake's campaign for the White House.

The head of D-PAC was Elaine Tyner, a lawyer from an enormous Washington firm. She knew everyone in Washington and people near the top of most foreign governments. She could raise millions of dollars and provide important information for Lake through the whole campaign. She also knew how to put money into people's pockets to guarantee support for him.

The campaign was going according to plan. Lake's advertisements were very successful: nobody liked them, and people now recognized Aaron Lake's face. He attracted even more attention when he made an unbelievable claim in an early interview.

"We expect to have $20 million in two weeks," Lake said calmly. Teddy Maynard had guaranteed him that the money would be there. Follow the money, and you'll find your winner, was the message.

"It's dirty money," Senator Britt of Maryland, the strongest of the seven other candidates in the presidential race, told reporters. "No honest candidate can raise so much money so quickly."

The CIA had a file on almost every senator and congressman in Washington, and the file on Britt was very interesting. His campaign was based on the idea of family values and low taxes, but he never told the voters, or his wife and five children, the facts about several trips he'd made to Southeast Asia nine years earlier.

On the first trip, with a group of senators, Britt met a beautiful young Thai woman from the American Embassy in Bangkok. A bit of excitement turned into a love affair and Britt returned to Thailand four more times, using American tax dollars to pay for everything. On the final trip, the young woman informed her lover that she was going to have his baby. He left Thailand as quickly as possible and never communicated with his "friend" again.

Britt forgot about his adventure, but Teddy Maynard didn't. Teddy didn't like Senator Britt and his frequent criticism of the CIA. So Teddy's men in Bangkok added information to Britt's file: pictures of Britt with his Thai girlfriend; medical reports on the baby which proved that Senator Britt was the father; credit card bills, and a recent photo of the boy, who looked a lot like the other Britt children.

Teddy instructed a CIA man to follow the Britt campaign and get close to the people at the top. Over a late drink, the CIA man, pretending to be a reporter, suggested that Senator Britt give up his attempt to become president. After hearing about the Thailand adventure, Britt's people agreed.

Senator Britt held a press conference the next day. He was out of the race for the White House. He wanted to spend more time with his family.

That afternoon, Teddy Maynard had a short, but important

meeting in his office with a man named Lufkin who'd been in the CIA for more than twenty years. Lufkin's information was secret and could only be delivered in person.

"There's going to be a bomb attack on our embassy in Cairo very soon," Lufkin reported. "It'll happen unless we take action."

"Go to Cairo and wait for the ground to shake," instructed Teddy. "Stay away from the embassy." Sometimes terror was necessary to get the right result.

Teddy Maynard finished his meeting with Lufkin and then showed York the next Aaron Lake TV advertisements. The new ones were full of blood and American bodies. And after each scene of death and horror, the viewers heard the voice of the American President of the time, promising revenge.

At the end, the handsome but serious face of Aaron Lake appeared on the screen, looked sincerely at the camera, and said, "The fact is, we don't take action. We shout and threaten, but in reality we bury our dead and forget about them. When I'm your president, no American death will be forgotten. We will destroy people who murder innocent Americans."

"The public won't like it," York said.

Just wait, Teddy told himself. Wait until there are more bodies. What will the public like, or even demand, then?

◆

Trevor was sitting in his little office drinking a large coffee when the call came.

"Mr. Carson? This is Mr. Brayshears at Nassau Trust Bank. I'm phoning to inform you that $100,000 was placed in your account this morning," said the banker in his attractive British accent.

"I'll come down to see you this afternoon. Thanks for phoning."

Trevor danced around his office and then hurried to the airport to catch the next plane to the Bahamas. He went directly to the bank and moved $25,000 of the money to his own account and received $8,000 in cash. He considered staying on the beach for a few days, but he knew he should visit Trumble as soon as possible.

◆

After his quick meeting with Trevor, Joe Roy Spicer almost ran to the prison library to find the other two judges.

"Trevor just left," he told them. "We got the $100,000 from old Quince in Iowa!"

"Where's the money?" asked Beech, closing his book.

"It was sent to our account in Nassau, as instructed."

"Let's hit him again," said Yarber, before the others could think of it. "We've got nothing to lose. Let's demand another $50,000."

The scam had now produced some real money, and the smell of cash made the three judges drunk with excitement. They began reading all the old letters and writing new ones. They wanted more pen pals, more money. More advertisements would be placed in the back pages of gay magazines.

Back in Neptune Beach, Trevor sat in Pete's Bar and dreamed his own dreams. He needed a million dollars, nothing more or less. Just one million dollars, and he could close his sad little office, surrender his law license, buy a boat, and spend the rest of his life sailing with the winds around the Caribbean.

He was closer than he'd ever be.

Joe Roy Spicer was thinking about Trevor at that exact moment. There was some serious cash in the Brethren's account in the Bahamas now, and they couldn't stop Trevor from stealing it.

The idea of a drunken lawyer walking away with all of their money was driving Joe Roy crazy. He lay in bed and tried to think of a way to make the scam work without the lawyer.

◆

Finn Yarber's wife, Carmen Topolski, arrived unannounced at Trumble, her first visit in ten months. She'd been married to Finn

22

for thirty years, but they hadn't always lived together. They were products of the sixties and believed in free love and social and political justice for everyone. As lawyers, they'd worked for people with few advantages and usually very little money.

But that was all in the past. Now both Carmen and Finn were tired of "the fight" and tired of each other. Carmen was at Trumble because she had some personal business to discuss.

"I want to end our marriage. There's someone new in my life, and I want to marry him."

"Show me the papers. I'll sign them," Finn said pleasantly.

"They'll be here in a week. It won't take long. We don't have anything to argue about, since we don't have anything these days," Carmen explained.

Nothing, that is, except Finn's growing fortune from the pen-pal scam. He'd be happy to see his money safely out of Carmen's reach. Show him the papers, he'd be very happy to sign.

It was the last visit Finn Yarber ever had from his wife.

Chapter 5   Life Gets Complicated

Lufkin was in Cairo again, sitting at a fashionable outdoor café, enjoying a strong black coffee. With his dark hair, expensive clothes, and perfect Arabic, he seemed like any other wealthy Arab businessman.

As Lufkin began his walk back through Garden City to the Hotel El-Nil on the edge of the Nile River, he was joined by a tall, thin man. They greeted each other like business contacts.

Then, as they walked along together, the man said, "Tonight's the night. There's a party at the embassy. Lots of traffic. The bomb will be in a van." The man left as suddenly as he'd appeared.

At 8 P.M., a large van from a popular Cairo restaurant drove through the gates of the American Embassy. The van parked near the service entrance to the building.

At 10:20, a 1,500-kilo bomb blew up the van and destroyed half of the embassy building. The explosion damaged buildings and cracked windows within half a kilometer.

Lufkin, sitting in his hotel room, jumped to his feet and ran to the window. The roof of the embassy was covered in flames. Fire engines were racing toward the scene. Cairo was dark except for the light from the fire at the American Embassy.

Teddy answered Lufkin's call on a safe line in his Langley office. "Yes, Maynard here."

"I'm in Cairo, Teddy. Watching our embassy go up in smoke," reported Lufkin.

Teddy moved to another phone and called Aaron Lake on his special line. The candidate was on his way from Philadelphia to Atlanta, traveling in his shiny new airplane.

"Mr. Lake, listen carefully, I have some important news. They bombed the American Embassy in Cairo fifteen minutes ago."

"Who?"

"Don't ask that. There will be reporters waiting for you when you get to Atlanta. Prepare your remarks. Express concern for the dead and for their families. People will remember your advertisements now. They'll remember how you've promised to react to situations like this one. Call me when you get to Atlanta."

Forty minutes later, Lake's plane landed and the congressman was met by an eager group of reporters and photographers. He spoke without notes: "At this moment, our thoughts and prayers are for those who have been injured or killed by this act of war. For them and for their families. When I am president, there will be fast and effective action. We will not allow these madmen to kill innocent Americans and then walk away."

Excellent, thought Teddy, as he watched from his office. Quick, caring, but firm and in control. He congratulated himself again for finding such a wonderful candidate.

Lufkin called Teddy again around 11 P.M. Washington time to report that the bodies of America's top official in Egypt and his wife had been found. That brought the total to eighty-four dead; seventy-three were Americans.

While talking to Lufkin, a Lake advertisement appeared on one of Teddy's screens. It showed a scene after a different explosion in another part of the world. Fifty Americans had died in that one. Then the smooth, sincere voice of Aaron Lake promised revenge.

What perfect timing, Teddy thought.

All of the presidential candidates got themselves on TV the next morning. All of them were calling for action against the terrorists. Their messages were beginning to sound like one of Aaron Lake's campaign advertisements.

♦

It was snowing again in Bakers, Iowa, and once again Quince Garbe thought of the Caribbean and his ruined dreams. With his head down, he rushed into the post office to check his private box.

One of those letters was waiting for him. His face burned with guilt and shame. He looked over his shoulder like a thief and then quickly removed the letter and pushed it deep into his coat pocket.

Quince ignored the bank, drove home, and hurried through the empty house. He ran to his bedroom and tore open the envelope.

Dear Quince

Thanks so much for the money. You'll be happy to know that it went to my wife and kids. They don't have anything. Another $50,000 would improve their life even more.

Same rules as before. Same promises to tell everyone about your secret if the money isn't received quickly.

Do it now, Quince, and I swear this is my last letter.

Love, Ricky

This was impossible. Quince had begged and even lied to borrow the $100,000 for Ricky. He couldn't find another $50,000.

25

The idea of death was almost pleasant. No more marriage, no more bank, no more Dad, no more Bakers, Iowa, no more hiding his real feelings. But he couldn't hurt his children and grandchildren.

He lay on the bedroom floor and thought about his situation—he wasn't even brave enough to mess up the bed. He didn't know how, but he had to find the money. He had to keep his secret until his father died. The old man couldn't last much longer. Then he'd have the bank and the money and could live as he pleased.

He must not take any chances with the money.

◆

Curtis V. Cates, Ricky's pen pal in Texas, was really Vann Gates, 58-year-old husband, father of three, grandfather of two, owner of six jewelry stores in the Dallas area.

Sometimes Vann had made careful arrangements for quick, secret sex, but his letters to Ricky were his first attempt to find the kind of love that he dreamed about.

Like Quince, he'd rented a private post-office box and was walking on air every time he received a letter from his sweet Ricky. But then, one day, he received the Brethren's usual deal: send $100,000 to a bank in the Bahamas, or your wife and family will know everything.

For a man who had carefully lived a double life, the money wouldn't be an enormous problem, but the letter broke Vann's heart. He'd have to finish his days with a woman he didn't love, in a life without honesty or excitement.

◆

Aaron Lake was on his private airplane again, watching the sad ceremony at Andrews Air Force Base. The seventy-three American bodies had returned home. Each name was read aloud, a band played, the families cried, and both the President and the Vice President spoke. The Vice President, the only candidate for the White House from the other big political party, made wild promises about finding the terrorists and getting justice.

When the Vice President finally finished, Lake looked around the plane. There were thirteen staff members with him. A private man who still missed his wife, Lake wished for a little time on his own, but these days he always moved in a group. They were always preparing for the next event in his busy schedule.

Just get to the White House, Lake told himself, and one day he'd sit in the president's office, alone, with the world at his feet. Then he could have a private life.

◆

Teddy and York sat in Teddy's office and watched the bodies arrive from Egypt, too. They'd shared many similar sad moments over the years. The Lake campaign would be Teddy's final effort at saving American lives.

Failure didn't seem possible. D-PAC had collected more than $20 million in two weeks and had talked to twenty-one congressmen who'd support Lake for President, at a total cost of $6 million. But D-PAC's biggest prize was Senator Britt, former candidate and father of a Thai boy. D-PAC paid off his $4-million campaign debt, and Senator Britt began giving loud, frequent, enthusiastic support to Aaron Lake's campaign.

The next stage in the presidential race was the day on which voters in Michigan and Arizona chose their candidate for the November election. Lake's ads—and the fact that the public had not forgotten the Cairo disaster—did their job. No one had ever started so late and come so far so fast; Lake was now the strongest candidate from either of the two big political parties.

The campaign plane landed in Washington, and Lake arrived at his Georgetown house at midnight. Guards were on duty outside, but he'd refused to have any inside the house.

As soon as the door was locked, Lake went upstairs to his bedroom and changed into his running clothes. He turned out the lights, waited fifteen minutes, then walked quietly through the dark house. He climbed through a window at the back and hurried to M Street. Quickly finding a taxi, the candidate drove off into the crowded city.

Teddy Maynard had been very satisfied that night with his candidate's victories in two big states. But he woke up the next morning to some extraordinary news. Something had gone wrong.

Sam Deville, the CIA man in charge of watching Lake's house, knew everything the candidate did when he was in the Washington area. He didn't have people inside the house, but there were listening devices in every room and on every door and window. There were also devices in the bottoms of every pair of Lake's shoes. Deville and his men always knew where Lake was when he was in their neighborhood.

"At 12:17 this morning Mr. Lake left his house through a window," Deville reported. "We had people following him before he got to M Street. He took a taxi to a shopping center in Chevy Chase and got out at Mailbox America, one of those new places where you can pick up mail twenty-four hours a day. Lake went inside and used a key to open his box, removed some envelopes, looked at them, threw them in the wastebasket, then returned to the taxi. He went directly home, climbed through the window at 1:22 and went to bed. He's still at home now."

"What about the envelopes?" asked Teddy.

"Nothing interesting. Mostly advertisements. But the address on the envelopes is Al Konyers, Box 455, Mailbox America."

"What was he looking for?" Teddy demanded.

"No clues yet, but we've connected a special device to box 455, and we've made a key for the lock. We'll know if anything goes in or out of that box," said Deville.

"Why does Lake need a private address and a false name?"

"We missed something," admitted York. "Maybe there's a girlfriend we didn't find out about. Or maybe he likes dirty videos and has them sent to the box."

"But if he rented the box before the campaign," Teddy

worried, "he's not hiding something from us, he's hiding something from the whole world, and his secret must be really terrible."

The three men looked at each other. No one wanted to guess Aaron Lake's secret. They decided to check the mailbox twice a day and have a CIA man watch it all day, every day.

Chapter 6   The Lake Mess

Trevor Carson was drinking too much every evening at Pete's, but these days he always seemed to have something to celebrate. He followed Spicer's advice on betting, and in the previous week he'd won $5,500 for himself.

That Monday morning, he had another phone call from Mr. Brayshears in the Bahamas.

"We've received another payment of $100,000 into your account, sir," reported the rather formal banker.

Trevor was in Mr. Brayshear's office before three o'clock that afternoon. The money had come from Curtis in Dallas, as expected. Once again, Trevor put $25,000 into his own account and $8,000 into his pocket. Then he went to a good hotel on the beach and got a room. He spent two days lying in the sun, drinking expensive drinks—brought to him by a beautiful waitress—and checking the local papers for the cost of used sailboats.

On Thursday morning, Trevor finally made it back to Trumble.

"Where've you been?" complained Joe Roy. "I've missed betting on three games, and I picked three winners."

Spicer's mood changed when he heard about the $100,000 from Curtis. He was $22,000 richer and his thoughts returned to the pen-pal scam. He gave Trevor a pile of letters to mail and his choices for ten more basketball games, putting $500 on each game.

The Brethren were glad to see Trevor leave that day. With about $50,000 each in the Nassau account, the judges wanted some time to plan the future which they now felt certain that they had. Back in their own rooms, each man added up how much money he could earn from the scam by the time he left prison. Their plans would mean more letters from Ricky, but also more exercise, fewer cigarettes, and healthier food. The judges intended to leave Trumble one day and be able to enjoy their riches.

◆

The next letter from Quince Garbe in Iowa was read aloud by Beech: "'*Dear Ricky (but I know that's not your real name): I don't have that much money. I had to lie and beg to get the $100,000. My father owns our bank and all its money. I might be able to get $10,000, but even that will be very difficult. Don't push me. I'm thinking about killing myself—then you'd get nothing. I hope the police catch you. Sincerely, Quince Garbe.*'"

◆

During the busy lunch period at Mailbox America in Chevy Chase, one of Deville's men checked box 455 for the second time that day. There were some advertisements as usual, but lying on top of them was a pale blue envelope addressed to Al Konyers.

An hour later, Deville, York, and Teddy Maynard were looking at a copy of the letter on one of Teddy's big screens and trying to understand what they called the "Lake mess."

Dear Al

Where've you been? I wrote three weeks ago and I haven't heard a word. I get very lonely here, and your letters keep me going because I know you really care.

I get out of here in two months and plan to go to Baltimore, near where I grew up, but everyone I used to know there is dead now. I need friends desperately, Al.

I've lost another couple of kilos and I've been exercising in the gym every day. I'll send you a new photograph. I think my face looks better now, without the baby fat. I wish you'd send a picture of you.

Please don't forget me, Al. I need your letters.

Love, Ricky

"Where did the letter come from?" asked Teddy.

"The address on the envelope says: Ricky, The Aladdin Drug Center, Box 44683, Neptune Beach, Florida, but the place doesn't exist. There isn't a drug center in Neptune Beach, and no one at any of the real drug centers in the whole Jacksonville area has ever heard of the Aladdin Center," said Deville.

"There are other letters, obviously, and at least one photograph," interrupted Teddy. "We have to find them. Lake is in California this week. Go over every centimeter of his house."

Teddy and York began working on a letter to send to Ricky.

Dear Ricky

Forgive me for not writing sooner. I've been traveling a lot lately. In fact, I just returned from Tampa. I'm in my office, trying out my new computer.

Wonderful news about getting out of the Aladdin Center. I have some business interests in Baltimore, and I'm sure I can help you find a job.

Don't be discouraged. I'll help in any way possible. Remember, you do have a friend.

I can't wait to hear from you again.

Love, Al

York printed the letter on writing paper from an expensive hotel in New Orleans and then placed it in a thick, plain brown envelope with a very tiny device hidden in one corner. The CIA could follow the signal from the device from a hundred meters. They put post marks on the envelope, and one of Deville's special agents carried the piece of mail to the post office in Neptune Beach. It took the agent, an expert in locks and keys, less than forty seconds to open box 44683 and place the envelope inside.

Three other agents waited patiently in a van in the parking lot, drinking coffee and videoing every customer to the post office. They were seventy meters away from the box, and their equipment was picking up the signal from the brown envelope.

They found the person who had rented the box after lunch.

Trevor had had lunch at Pete's: a few beers and some peanuts from the bowl on the bar. He returned to his office and slept for an hour before walking over to the post office. He was delighted to see four letters to Ricky in the Aladdin Center's box. More letters meant more money.

Seven CIA agents watched him as he returned to his office.

◆

Deville delivered a full report on Trevor Carson that evening: age forty-eight, two former wives, no children ... The information covered several pages. Then Teddy Maynard came to something unusual: this lazy, unsuccessful lawyer visited Trumble Federal Prison at least three times a week. Sometimes four. All of his visits were official lawyer–client conferences.

"Who is his client in this prison?" asked Teddy.

"It's not Ricky. He's the lawyer for three judges," reported Deville.

"Three judges in prison?" asked Teddy.

"Yes. They call themselves the Brethren. We followed him to Trumble yesterday, and when he came out we couldn't pick up the signal from our device in the envelope to Ricky. He went directly to Pete's Bar and Grill and stayed there for three hours. We searched his car and there were eight letters from Ricky addressed to men all over the country. It seems that Trevor Carson's job is to carry mail to and from his clients. Thirty minutes ago he was still in the bar, quite drunk, betting on basketball games."

While Trevor stayed in Pete's, a team of CIA agents copied the contents of his briefcase and put listening devices in the case, in his car, his office, and his house. The next morning several agents with a load of technical equipment moved into an apartment across the street from Trevor's office. Now, no matter where Trevor Carson went, the CIA would be watching and listening.

Trevor's visits to the Brethren were always in the afternoon, and he always went from the prison to Pete's. This gave the CIA men time to check and copy any letters that he brought back from Trumble. The CIA experts soon knew that Hatlee Beech and Finn Yarber were writing letters to men all over the country.

Teddy studied each letter from Ricky and almost admired Beech and Yarber's approach. They let Ricky talk about the drug problems in his past and his hopes and dreams for the future. He always wrote about his desperate need for a friend that he could trust and spend time with. He was proud that he was finished with drugs, and he was proud of his healthy body, which was getting browner and harder every day. It was a flesh game—a strong young body available for friendship—and Teddy's candidate was caught in the middle of it.

There were still questions, but Teddy was patient. They'd watch the mail. The pieces would fall into place.

Chapter 7   Who's in Control?

The President appeared on TV to announce that US intelligence knew who had placed the bomb at the American Embassy in Cairo. He informed the public that he'd ordered an air attack on a terrorist group, in and around the city of Talah in Tunisia.

The American people sat in front of their TV sets and watched and waited. But the smart bombs weren't smart enough. They hit the terrorists' main buildings and destroyed them, but the buildings were empty and no terrorists were killed. A couple of smart bombs missed their goal, however, and hit the center of Talah. They destroyed a small hospital and a house next to it. Forty-seven very innocent people were dead.

Suddenly, the President and the Vice President could not be found to speak on TV to the American people. The only man who spoke confidently after the Talah bombings was Aaron Lake.

"We should be ashamed of these mistakes. You can't just push buttons and then hide your head. When I am president, we will be prepared. No terrorist with American blood on his hands will be safe. I will act quickly and accurately. I will take responsibility."

People believed Aaron Lake. He was the man.

◆

Hatlee Beech opened the brown envelope without noticing that the right lower corner was a bit fat and slightly damaged.

"Who's Al Konyers?" Finn asked, looking at the letter.

Hatlee checked his file and said, "We don't know much about him. He lives in the Washington area. Uses a mailbox service. This is his third letter. Here's the first one from December 11."

Dear Ricky
   Hello. My name is Al Konyers. I'm in my fifties. I like guitar music, old movies, and I read modern novels. I don't smoke and don't like people who do. A fun evening for me is Chinese food, a little wine, an old movie on the video with a good friend. I hope you'll write.

                                                              Al Konyers

The letter showed that Al was nervous about making contact with Ricky. He didn't give any personal information and didn't even sign his name.

The Brethren sent him the photo and their usual first letter from Ricky. It included some questions to get Al to talk about himself, but his second letter to Ricky was still short and cautious. He did say, however, that he worked for the government and was not married. Al wasn't very interesting to the Brethren. There wasn't a wife who would be upset to find out that Al was gay, and probably only a fairly low salary from a government job. He was too careful, and, therefore, too much hard work for the Brethren.

But when Finn and Hatlee read Al's third letter—written by Teddy Maynard and York—they noticed something different.

"I think Al Konyers has been thinking about Ricky," said Finn.

"Yeah. He sounds excited about the idea of meeting him," agreed Hatlee. "But does he have any money?"

"He talks about 'business interests in Baltimore'—he must be doing OK. And if he works for the government, he won't want people to know that he has a gay pen pal."

"Let's try another letter and see how he reacts. He might be a good candidate for $100,000. What've we got to lose?"

Beech wrote:

Dear Al

Thanks for your last letter. I feel like I've been living in a cage for months, but your letters help to open the door.

I have a great idea. In two months, when I get out of here, let's rent a couple of Bogart films, get some Chinese food and a bottle of non-alcoholic wine, and spend a quiet evening on the sofa.

There are a lot of things I miss in here, and not just drugs and good food. You can probably guess what I mean.

I really will need a job when I get to Baltimore. If you can arrange something, I will be very grateful.

Please write soon, Al. Your letters really help when I am feeling low. Thanks, friend.

Love, Ricky

35

Finn Yarber finished another letter to Quince Garbe:

> Dear Quince
>   Ten thousand is not enough. I'll take $25,000 and not a penny
> less. Send the money now, Quince, or you know what will happen.
>   Love, Ricky

For his next visit to Teddy Maynard, the presidential candidate
arrived in a big black van with a driver and several bodyguards.
The two men shook hands warmly and appeared happy to see
each other.

They discussed Lake's recent victories and planned the next
two important stages in the presidential race: Big Tuesday and
Little Tuesday, which would cover more than a quarter of the
whole country. The polls showed that Lake was ahead by at least
five points in every state.

They enjoyed talking about the election for a few more
minutes, then Teddy turned serious.

"Two nights ago," he said, and the smile was gone, "in the
mountains of Afghanistan, about $30 million worth of Russian
military weapons was moved by truck into Pakistan. It's now on
its way to Iran. The Iranians paid the money into an account in
Luxembourg that is controlled by Natty Chenkov's people."

"Why is Chenkov selling weapons?" asked Lake.

"He'll use the money to buy more modern weapons and
power."

Teddy rolled his wheelchair closer to Lake.

"Listen to me, Mr. Lake," he said in a sad, serious voice. "The
Russians will threaten us soon. Our country needs you as
president, and you're going to win the election. Keep the message
simple: our freedom is at risk, the world is not as safe as it looks. If
we told the public about that equipment in Afghanistan, do you
think they'd be worried about higher taxes? I'll take care of the
fear, Mr. Lake. You stay out of trouble and work hard on the
campaign."

"I'm working as hard as I can," Aaron Lake said sincerely.

"Work harder, and no surprises, OK?"

"Absolutely not."

♦

Two CIA agents were sent to Bakers, Iowa to find the younger Mr. Garbe. They told Quince's secretary that they were bank inspectors from the federal government. Quince couldn't refuse to see them.

In his office, the nervous banker asked, "What can we do for you, gentlemen?"

"Is the door locked?" asked Chap, one of the agents.

"Yes—yes, it is," said Quince, who looked like he'd been crying. He spent most of his life behind locked doors, worrying about his problems.

"We're not banking officials, Mr. Garbe. We know some things about you, about letters and trips to the Caribbean, about Ricky."

"Who are you?" whispered Quince, in terror.

"Let's say that we have a client that Ricky is hurting, too. We want to protect him and you can help."

"No, I can't do anything," said Quince shyly.

"It's going to be easy," said Chap, as he placed a thick envelope on Quince's desk. "There's $25,000 in cash. Send it to Ricky."

Quince was so confused that his brain hurt. Why were these men offering him money? How much did they know about him?

"Send the money and your problem is solved."

"Is that all I have to do?" asked Quince.

"Give us all the information you have on Ricky. Show us your letters. Show us everything," said Wes, the second agent.

"But will my secret be safe with you?" asked Quince.

"There's no reason for us to tell anyone about you. We're only worried about our client."

"Can you make Ricky stop?"

"We intend to put Ricky out of business."

Quince looked at the money and said in a shaky voice, "Then I have no choice."

He opened a secret drawer in his desk and gave the two men everything: the magazine with Ricky's advertisement; the photo; the letters; the two tickets for a Caribbean vacation.

As the CIA agents looked through the papers on the desk, Quince's head began to clear and he began to see the end of his worries. He wouldn't have to lie and beg to find $25,000. It was on his desk, waiting to be sent, and these two big, strong men would get rid of Ricky for him. Quince was almost thinking of these men as his friends. In fact, he thought, he was having a conversation with the first two people in his life who knew he was gay. It was a strange and exciting experience.

"How will you stop Ricky?" he asked boldly.

"We'll probably just kill him," said Chap.

Quince began to smile. His secret was safe, and one day he'd be free.

"How nice," he said softly. "How very nice."

At the same time, other CIA agents were working on other areas of the "Lake mess." They had the records of both the Brethren's and Trevor's bank accounts in the Bahamas; they knew about Curtis Cates and several other pen pals, and they had almost fifty people watching Aaron Lake all the time.

"We must watch him," Teddy told York. "He isn't the person we thought he was. He might write another letter to Ricky or buy another one of those magazines."

"What about putting someone in Trumble Prison?" suggested York. "We need to know if the Brethren know who Al Konyers really is."

"Get Deville to work on it. It's a good idea," said Teddy.

"And, we need a letter from Ricky to Lake so we can follow it and find out if Lake has a 'Ricky file,'" said York.

"Excellent. Get Deville on that, too."

"Are you going to tell Lake that you know about Ricky?" asked York.

"Not yet. Maybe this gay thing only happened after his wife died. If Ricky is his only secret, maybe we can keep it quiet."

"Did we pick the wrong man?" asked York.

"No," said Teddy Maynard. "Those three judges picked the wrong man."

◆

York was walking his dog on Sunday and suddenly had another good idea: use the pen-pal scam on the Brethren. The CIA would create a new pen pal for Ricky and move attention away from Al Konyers. There was nothing to lose.

The letter-writing experts at Langley started work and Brant White was born. He wrote Ricky a letter on expensive cream-colored paper:

Dear Ricky

I liked your advertisement. I'm fifty-five, in great shape, and looking for more than a pen pal. My wife and I just bought a home in Palm Valley, near Neptune Beach. We'll be down in three weeks, with plans to stay for two months.

If interested, send photograph.

Brant

Trevor was going to Trumble almost every afternoon now. He usually had five or six letters for Joe Roy and collected as many as ten from him.

Spicer opened the letter from Brant White. "Oh, a new pen pal. What kind of place is Palm Valley?"

"It's one of those expensive neighborhoods with gates and guards. I've seen houses in Palm Valley advertised for $3 million. Why?" asked Trevor.

"Wait here. I'm going to the library. I'll be back in half an hour."

Joe Roy Spicer rushed into the conference room and shouted, "Stop your work. We've finally got a big one. Look at this," and he threw Brant White's letter on the table. "This old boy's got plenty of cash, and he wants to come down in three weeks."

Hatlee and Finn worked quickly and produced a typical first letter from Ricky, but shorter than usual. He said he'd be leaving the drug center in ten days, and then living with a sister in Jacksonville. He'd be ready for Brant when he traveled south. Would Brant's wife be in Palm Valley, too? Wouldn't it be great if she stayed in Pennsylvania?

They finished the letter and put in the same color photograph they'd used a hundred times. Most of the pen pals fell in love as soon as they saw the photograph.

The pale blue envelope was taken by Spicer back to the visitors' room where Trevor was sleeping.

"Mail this immediately," Spicer shouted at him. Trevor was on his way to Pete's in a couple of minutes.

◆

March 7. Big Tuesday. Aaron Lake celebrated victory after victory as the results from each state were announced. By the time the votes were counted in California, Lake had captured 390 of the 591 state votes that had been available. All bets were on Lake.

The next morning in California, Lake gave eighteen live interviews in two hours, then flew to Washington. He met with his team of well-paid campaign workers and learned that he had $65 million and no debts. His strongest rival had less than $1 million and a mountain of debts. Lake was getting all the money.

"Mr. Lake," the campaign director said, "the press will want to know everything about you now. You're new and they haven't tried to find any dirt on you yet. It's time for them to get nasty."

"Don't worry," Lake said. "I have nothing to hide." Then he went home for the first time in days.

The D-PAC team was also busy. They were spending $60,000 a week on polls and knew how well Aaron Lake would do in every state. They were also designing more TV advertisements and spending lots of money to guarantee enormous support from senators and congressmen. Elaine Tyner was having a great time.

"It's amazing what a few million dollars can do," she laughed. "We'll raise $60 million and spend every penny by election day in November."

◆

Back at Langley, a team of experts began working on a letter from Ricky to Al Konyers. They copied Ricky's handwriting, his style, and his pen and paper.

The letter said:

Hey, Al, where have you been? Why haven't you written? Don't forget about me.

But there was also a nice little surprise. Since Ricky couldn't use the phone at the center, he was sending Al a cassette tape. Its purpose was to carry a small device that would send out a signal to the CIA agents. This should lead them to Lake's private "Ricky file" if there was one.

At Mailbox America in Chevy Chase, the CIA now controlled eight boxes. Agents came and went into the building during both the day and night, checking their boxes and looking into box 455 to see if there was anything new for Al Konyers.

The agents knew Aaron Lake's schedule and knew he was at home in Georgetown for one night. They put the envelope with the cassette tape in box 455 at ten o'clock that night.

As expected, at two in the morning Aaron Lake climbed out of the same back window, with a dozen CIA agents watching him, found a taxi, and went to Mailbox America. He rushed in, pulled out his mail, and hurried back to the waiting car.

Six hours later, Aaron Lake left Georgetown for a flight to Dallas and another busy week of campaigning.

By the time Lake's plane was in the air, a team of CIA agents was in his house. Their search did not last long. They followed the signal and found the cassette tape from Ricky in the wastebasket in Lake's kitchen. It was mixed in with the other garbage which would be thrown out by the cleaner who came in twice a week.

It looked like Mr. Lake was a smart man; he simply threw away his mail from Ricky. He hid his secret life very well.

Actually, Ricky's tape had made Aaron Lake nervous. He'd enjoyed receiving Ricky's letters and looking at his handsome face. He didn't intend to meet the young man, but he thought a pen-pal relationship would be safe and exciting at the same time.

Then he received the tape, and the sound of Ricky's voice brought him close and made the game too dangerous. The possibility of someone finding out about Ricky was much too risky. He didn't think he'd get caught. He was hidden behind the post office and "Al Konyers," and Ricky didn't have any idea about who he really was. But it had to end. At least for now.

Sitting alone for a few minutes in his private plane, surrounded by a team of campaign workers, Lake drank his tomato juice and decided to write a final letter to Ricky and simply say goodbye.

He wanted to write the letter there and then, but he was interrupted every minute or two by someone with another report or a new poll or a decision to be made.

Surely he'd be able to hide in the White House. Presidents were allowed to have a private life, weren't they?

Chapter 8   Buster and Brant

At the most recent meeting of the "Lesser Court of Northern Florida," the Brethren settled a case about a stolen cell phone. When everyone had gone, one young man remained in his chair.

"Who are you?" Spicer asked the quiet kid.

The boy looked at the three judges in their pale green church robes, and said nervously, "Everyone calls me Buster. I got here last week and my roommate said you could probably help me."

"Don't you have a lawyer?" Beech asked.

"I did. He wasn't very good. He's one reason I'm here."

"Did you have a trial?" asked Spicer.

"Yes. A long one."

"And you were found guilty by a jury?"

"Yes. Me and my dad and a bunch of other guys. They said we were smuggling drugs into the United States from South America."

Drugs. Suddenly, the Brethren were anxious to get back to their letter writing.

"How long is your sentence?" asked Yarber.

"Forty-eight years."

The letter writing was forgotten for the moment. The three men looked at the sad young face and tried to picture it fifty years later. Even Spicer felt a little sympathetic toward the boy.

"OK, Buster, what did you do to get forty-eight years?"

The story poured out of the innocent-looking young man. He and his father had a small business in Pensacola, repairing boats and selling fishing equipment. It was the perfect life for them. They sold a used twenty-meter fishing boat to a man for $95,000 in cash. Cash for boats was not unusual in Florida. But after the fifth boat, federal agents came for a visit. They threatened Buster and his dad and wanted to see their bank accounts. Buster's dad hired a lawyer and he advised them not to cooperate. Nothing happened for months.

The federal agents came back for Buster and his father at 3 A.M. on a Sunday morning. They had a 160-page document that named the two of them as part of a gang of twenty-five people, including the man who had bought boats from them. All were accused of smuggling large quantities of drugs into the United States.

At the trial, Buster and his father were alarmed to find themselves sitting at a table with the real drug smugglers. In seven weeks, their names were mentioned three times. They were accused of finding and repairing boats for the transport of drugs from Mexico to Florida.

Their own lawyer didn't make a separate case for his two clients. The jury saw Buster and his father as part of the gang and found all twenty-five men guilty of the same crime. A month after the decision, Buster's father killed himself.

Buster said, "I did nothing wrong." His eyes filled with tears.

A lot of men at Trumble claimed that they were innocent, but Buster was believable. Yarber and Beech pitied the young man.

But Spicer thought about the pen-pal scam and the possibility of a job for Buster. Joe Roy would be the first of the Brethren to leave Trumble, but the scam was too good to walk away from. Beech and Yarber could write letters, but they had no business sense. Maybe Spicer could train young Buster to take his place and to send his share of the money to the outside. Just an idea.

"Do you have any money?" Spicer asked.

"No, sir. We lost everything. I don't have a penny."

"I think we can help," Beech said. He was thinking about innocent people he had probably sent to prison. "We'll look at your case, but please don't be optimistic."

They left the cafeteria in a group: three former judges in green church robes followed by a scared young man. Frightened, but also quite curious.

◆

Brant White's reply to Ricky's first letter was quick and urgent:

Dear Ricky

What a photograph! I'm coming down to Florida even sooner than planned. I'll be there on April 20. Are you available? We can be alone in the house because my wife will stay here for another two weeks. We've been married for twenty-two years and she doesn't have a clue.

Here's a picture of me with my jet, one of my favorite toys. I'll take you for a little trip in it.

Write me immediately, please.

Sincerely, Brant

Spicer looked at the envelope for a minute and thought about how quickly the mail was running between Jacksonville and Philadelphia. But the photograph from Brant kept his attention. A handsome middle-aged man and woman, smiling, standing together in front of their private jet. It seemed odd to send a photograph with his wife, but nothing surprised Spicer anymore. He hurried off to find Yarber and Beech.

"Let's pull him in," Yarber said.

"How much?" asked Beech, still staring at the photograph.

"At least half a million," Spicer said. "And if we get that, we'll go back for more."

They sat in silence and thought about their growing bank account.

"Why is Trevor making so much with each deal?" Spicer asked.

"Yeah," Beech said. "We're doing the work, and he's getting more than each of us. I say we cut it."

"I'll do it on Thursday," said Spicer.

♦

Trevor Carson arrived at Trumble on Thursday afternoon after a heavy night of drinking at Pete's and had to face Joe Roy Spicer, who was ready for business. He handed an envelope to Trevor and said, "We're getting ready to demand money from this guy."

"Which one is he?" asked Trevor.

"Brant from around Philadelphia. He's hiding behind a post-office box, so you need to find out who he is."

"How much are we going for?"

"Half a million dollars."

Trevor's thoughts went to sailboats and Caribbean islands. He'd be $167,000 closer after this deal.

"And we're changing your share of the cash," said Spicer.

"You can't do that," Trevor argued. "I know too much."

"We know everything, too. But think about it. We're in jail already. If you tell everything, you'll be in here with us."

In his condition, Trevor couldn't argue with Spicer, and, anyway, they were talking about the difference between $167,000 and $125,000. Either amount sounded like a fortune to Trevor.

"OK," said Trevor, still in pain. "There's a good reason you're in prison."

"Are you drinking too much? You look awful," said Spicer. "We don't want a drunk for a lawyer. If you start talking too much in a bar, somebody could start asking questions."

"I can handle myself."

"Be careful. If I got one of our letters, I'd think about coming down here and finding some answers before I paid the money."

Trevor left Trumble and drove back to Neptune Beach. He sat in Pete's and thought about the Brethren. Between his account and their account, there was $250,000 in the Bahamas. Add a half a million to it, and, well, he couldn't stop adding: $750,000! He could take it all and be on a boat sailing between islands in the Caribbean. What could they do, sitting in jail?

"Stop it," he told himself.

He walked back to his office and began phoning private detectives in the Philadephia area. He had to find out who "Brant" really was. He got through to two answering machines and left messages. He tried a few more numbers, but it was already seven o'clock. He'd try again tomorrow.

Across the street, the CIA agents listened to the messages Trevor left on the answering machines in Philadelphia. Now they knew how the Brethren got the real names of Ricky's pen pals. Trevor simply hired local private detectives to do the work for him.

"This means that the lawyer could hire a local detective here to find out who Al Konyers really is," Deville said to Teddy.

"But how?" asked Teddy.

"Several ways. They could just watch the post office and catch Lake going in to check his box. Or they could pay someone at the post office for information. Or they could get the information from computer records."

"This lawyer's too dangerous," said Teddy.

"Kill him?" asked Deville.

"We'll buy him first. If he's working for us, we can keep him away from Al Konyers. Plan how to kill him, but not right away."

◆

The southern states loved Aaron Lake, with his talk of bombs and military spending. His bold advertisements were shown regularly in the south, and D-PAC spent a lot of money raising support in the region before Little Tuesday.

The results were very positive and Lake was a long way ahead of his closest rival. The race was over, if there were no surprises.

◆

Buster had an outside job at Trumble. He had to keep the sports areas neat and clean. He worked hard in the bright sun and promised himself that he'd stay in good shape while he was in prison. But after ten days Buster knew that he wouldn't last for forty-eight years.

He'd cried for the first forty-eight hours.

He was working near the basketball court when he saw Finn Yarber walking around the edge of the sports area.

Buster walked over and asked, "Can I join you?"

"Sure, Buster. How's it going?"

"I'm still here. I was wondering about my case."

"Judge Beech and I have looked into it. Everything was done legally, and it'd be difficult to get a new trial because it's a drug case. I'm sorry, Buster," said Yarber, and he meant it. He believed Buster was completely innocent.

Yarber looked off in the distance, to the edge of a small forest.

Buster looked, too. For ten days he'd been looking and seeing what wasn't there: fences, guard towers, watch dogs.

"The last guy who left here," Yarber said, "left through those trees."

"What happened to him?"

"He went crazy and walked away one day. He was gone for six hours before anybody knew it. A month later he was found sitting in the corner of a room in a cheap hotel, afraid to go outside. The hotel manager found him, not the police."

"Do many people walk away?"

"It happens about once a year. Most of them get caught because they do dumb things. They go home, they visit their girlfriends, they drive their cars too fast."

"So if you had a brain, you could get away?"

"With careful planning and a little cash, it'd be easy."

"Mr. Yarber, tell me something. If you were facing forty-eight years, would you take a walk?"

"Yes."

"But I don't have a penny."

"I do, but give it some time. They're watching you because you're new, but with time they'll forget about you."

Buster actually smiled. His sentence had just been reduced.

"You'd have to leave the country. Maybe South America. Do you have a girlfriend?"

"I think she's still my girlfriend, but I haven't heard from her since my trial," said Buster sadly.

"Forget about her. She'll only get you in trouble. Besides, did you expect her to wait forty-eight years for you? What about your mother or brothers and sisters?"

"It was just my dad and me. My mother died when I was a baby."

"You're the perfect guy to walk away. But keep quiet about it for now. Be patient. Let's plan it carefully."

"I'm ready when you say," Buster said. At that moment, he could see all the way to South America.

Chapter 9   The Trap Closes

As the presidential race went on, it became clear that Aaron Lake and Governor Tarry were the two most serious presidential candidates from their party. So by the beginning of May, a debate looked like a good idea for both sides. Governor Tarry was running out of money and needed some free TV time. Aaron Lake needed an opportunity to explain his position on taxes, federal spending, and social services, as well as on America's military strength. He was going to beat Tarry, but he wanted the public to see that he could also beat the Vice President in November.

There was a TV audience of eighteen million people for the first and only debate between Governor Tarry and Congressman Lake.

If Tarry was going to have any chance against Lake, he needed either an excellent performance by himself, or a really bad one by Lake. He got neither. In his opening remarks, he forgot to tell the listeners why he was a good candidate, and instead made a loud, nasty attack on Lake. He looked nervous and exhausted when he sat down.

Lake, on the other hand, was cool and confident. He ignored his rival and discussed important areas: taxes, business, jobs, education. Not a word about defense.

In his closing remarks, Tarry returned to Lake's plan to double military spending and tried to prove that it was unnecessary in times of peace. Lake stood up, looking very serious. He knew much more about this subject than Tarry did, and his final arguments made the governor sound like a schoolboy.

The polls, which were taken immediately after the debate, gave a solid win to Lake. Seventy percent of the audience thought he'd be a better president than Tarry.

On the late flight from Pittsburgh to Wichita, Aaron Lake and his team enjoyed a small victory party. More polls were coming in, and they all showed Lake as the clear winner in the debate.

During the celebration, Lake had two glasses of wine with the young workers around him. He thanked them and congratulated them, and they talked about the details of the debate. But the party didn't last long. Soon the lights were out and most of the campaign team were asleep.

Aaron Lake sat in his big leather chair but couldn't sleep. He took out his personal writing paper, with "Aaron Lake" printed at the top, and wrote a few notes to old friends.

Sometimes his notes went over one page, and he had some plain paper without his name, too. He checked to make sure everyone was asleep and quickly wrote a note on the plain paper:

> Dear Ricky
>   I think it's best if we stop writing letters to each other. I wish you well with your future.
>
>   Sincerely, Al

He wrote Ricky's address at Aladdin North on a plain envelope, and then he continued to write twenty thank-you notes to serious supporters before he felt sleepy. With the notes still in front of him and his reading light still on, the candidate fell asleep.

He'd slept less than an hour when loud voices awakened him. Alarm bells were ringing and there was smoke all around him.

The pilot announced that the plane was going to make an emergency landing in St. Louis. The lights went off and on and someone screamed. Lake had a minute or two to think. He quickly picked up his letters and envelopes and saw the letter to Ricky. He put it in the envelope to Aladdin North, closed it carefully, and put it into his case before the lights all went out for good.

This can't be happening, Lake told himself. I'm going to be President of the United States. I can't die now.

Then suddenly, the air turned cold and the smoke disappeared rapidly. From the windows they could see lights on the ground.

Soon the plane landed and the frightened passengers were rushing through the emergency doors. A fire was still burning in the back, and fire trucks surrounded the plane in seconds.

Lake hurried away with the others. He held tightly to his case with his letters inside, and for the first time went white with horror.

◆

Sam Deville and the CIA team working on the "Lake mess" wrote another letter to Ricky on the same personal computer. It read:

Dear Ricky

Good news about you coming to Baltimore. I think I have a job for you there. It's in an office, not a lot of money, but a good place to start.

Let's have lunch when you arrive. I'm not the type to rush into things.

Hope you're doing well. I'll write more about the job next week.

Best Wishes, Al

Only the "Al" was written by hand. Then the letter was flown and hand-delivered to Aladdin North's post box in Neptune Beach, where it sat for two days.

Trevor had been in Fort Lauderdale for a few days doing real lawyer work. On his return, he stopped at the post-office box and collected a pile of letters for Ricky. He went directly to Trumble, instead of going to Pete's Bar and Grill and giving the CIA men time to look through the mail while he had a few beers.

At Trumble, Spicer couldn't be found, so Trevor met with Beech. The lawyer left fourteen letters for the Brethren and took eight to mail in the morning.

"What about Brant in Philadelphia?" Beech asked, looking at the new envelopes.

"I'm still searching. I've been out of town, but I'll do it tomorrow." Trevor left in less than twenty minutes.

For Trevor, it was business as usual, but the Brethren were locked in their office in the library late into the night.

On the table were three letters. One was from Al's computer, sent two days earlier from Washington, D.C. One was Al's note in which he said he wanted to stop writing to Ricky, sent three days earlier from St. Louis. Different people had obviously written these two letters. Someone was playing with their mail.

They looked at the third letter and stopped to think about it. It was dated April 18, 1:20 A.M., and addressed to a woman named Carol.

Dear Carol
  What a great night! The debate couldn't have gone better. Thanks a million to you and your team. Let's keep working and winning! See you next week.

It was signed by Aaron Lake, and the writing paper had his name printed across the top. It was clearly written by the same person who had written the letter to Ricky from St. Louis.

The Brethren had studied the letters for almost five hours, and they were now certain that (a) the letter from the personal computer was not really from Al, but from someone who knew about their scam; (b) the notes to Ricky and Carol were written by hand by Aaron Lake; and (c) the note to Carol had been sent to them by mistake.

Above all, Al Konyers was really Aaron Lake. They'd caught the most famous politician in the country, after the President, in their little scam.

They went over all the facts. Konyers's mailbox was in the D.C. area. He'd typed all of his other letters and hadn't sent a photograph. After the big debate, Lake's airplane had made an emergency landing in St. Louis. He had too much to lose now and wanted to end things with Ricky. But why had he written this last letter by hand?

The letter to Carol had been written at 1:20 A.M. and the plane had landed at 2:15.

"He wrote it on the plane," Yarber said. "It was late and everyone was exhausted. He couldn't get to a computer."

"Then why not wait?" asked Spicer.

"He made a mistake. He probably thought he was being smart, but the letters got mixed up because of the trouble on the plane. Look at the big picture. He'd just performed wonderfully in a big debate on TV. He's going to win the election, but he's got Ricky. He takes care of his little secret, but then the plane catches fire. And now he's got an enormous problem. And he doesn't know it," Yarber added. "Yet."

But what about the typed letter from Al? Who had written that letter? Was it someone close to Lake who wanted to protect him?

They decided to have Trevor watch Al Konyers's mailbox in Chevy Chase and find out who was putting letters into it. Then they thought about Aaron Lake. He was rushing from one state to the next with his team of supporters and helpers. He had no time to think for himself.

And the Brethren had all day, hour after hour, to sit with their thoughts and plans. It was not an equal fight. Somehow, they were going to get Aaron Lake.

Chapter 10   Trevor Changes Jobs

At 1:30 P.M. Joe Roy Spicer lined up to use one of the safe telephone lines. Prisoners at Trumble could have private conversations on these lines with their lawyers.

After several rings, Trevor answered in a sleepy voice.

"Wake up, Trevor, and get to work. We need something done quickly," Joe Roy shouted.

The CIA agents in the apartment across the street were listening to every word. This was the first call they'd heard from Trumble.

"What is it?" asked Trevor.

"We need a mailbox checked out. Quickly. And we want you to go and do it. Don't leave until the job is finished."

"Why me?"

"Just do it, OK? This could be the biggest payday yet."

"OK. What do I do?" Trevor was getting interested now.

"Chevy Chase, Maryland. Write this down. Al Konyers, Box 455, Mailbox America, 39380 Western Road. Be very careful because this guy could have some powerful friends. Take some cash and hire some good detectives."

After the call, Trevor phoned the airport to find out about flights to Washington, D.C. CIA agents Wes and Chap walked across the street and entered Trevor's office. They didn't knock.

"Mr. Carson?"

"Yes, but my office is closed for today. Maybe you could come back next week."

Chap closed and locked the door behind him, then he took a gun from his jacket and pointed it at poor Trevor, whose heart froze.

"Just keep quiet, Mr. Carson, and listen," said Wes. "We have a client, a wealthy man, who's been caught by the little scam you and Ricky are running."

Trevor was shaking now.

"It's a wonderful idea," Wes said. "Blackmailing rich gay men who want to keep their love life a secret. They can't complain."

"Almost perfect," said Chap. "Until you catch the wrong fish, which is exactly what you've done this time."

"It's not my scam," Trevor said in a scared voice.

"But it wouldn't work without you, would it?" Wes asked. "Ricky needs you to carry the mail and take care of the money and do some detective work."

"Are you policemen? I'm not talking anymore if you're the police. I don't trust the police," Trevor said nervously.

"We're not the police. We come in peace. We want you on our

side," explained Wes. "We want to kill the scam from this office."

"You want me to lie to a client?" asked Trevor.

"Your client is a prisoner in a federal jail who's committing crimes every day. You're as guilty as he is. You can work for us, or you can join your client inside Trumble."

"Why doesn't your client just pay the blackmail money? That'd be a lot easier," suggested Trevor.

"But Ricky doesn't play fair, does he? If we paid him, then he'd come back for more. And more. Remember Quince Garbe?"

Trevor wondered how much they knew.

"Listen, Mr. Carson, we can offer you a very good deal."

Trevor had never really liked Spicer, and the Brethren had just cut his share of the money. "What's in it for me?" he asked.

"A hundred thousand dollars, cash," Chap said.

"My information is worth a million," Trevor said. "I'd have to leave the country. I'd never be able to work as a lawyer again."

Chap paused and then said, "Our client will pay a million."

And Trevor laughed. He was excited and couldn't stop laughing. Across the street, the CIA agents listened and laughed, too, because Trevor was laughing.

Trevor invited Wes and Chap to Pete's for lunch so they could work out the details of their deal. By the time Trevor had finished three beers and ordered one more to take with him, they'd agreed that he'd get one hundred thousand in cash and the rest of the money in his private account in the Bahamas. Then Trevor would tell them everything.

At five o'clock that afternoon, the Brethren's lawyer was holding a case with $100,000 inside. He looked at the money and laughed again. He'd crossed over to the other side.

The next morning, Trevor's new bosses, Chap and Wes, were at the door of his apartment at 7:30. They waited while he took a shower and dressed and then walked to his office with him. The CIA agents were now completely in charge of Trevor's life.

The first piece of business was to give Trevor the documents showing that the rest of the million dollars was now in his bank account in the Bahamas. Then they phoned the few clients Trevor had meetings with in the next thirty days and rescheduled them. Wes and Chap didn't want any interruptions.

Trevor quickly told them the names of the Brethren, and Wes and Chap did a wonderful job of acting surprised.

"Three judges?" they'd both repeated, sounding amazed.

Trevor smiled with great pride. He pretended to be the boss of the scam. He pretended that he'd persuaded three judges to work for him.

"Let's talk about Quince Garbe," Wes said. "How did you discover his real name?"

"I found a private detective in Des Moines, Iowa," Trevor said, drinking coffee, his feet on his desk, just like a very rich businessman. "He spent two days in Bakers and found a single mother with a few kids, old car, small apartment. She worked at the post office and was happy to give him the name of the person who was renting box 788 in exchange for $500."

"Do you always get your information from inside?"

"No, sometimes I hire someone to watch the post office. When we see a guy collect his mail, we can find out who he is by his car license plates."

"Who's next?" asked Wes.

"Probably this guy who lives near Philadelphia. He's using the name Brant White. He's got plenty of money," Trevor said.

"Do you ever read the letters?"

"Never. I don't want to know what's in them. And I don't keep anything here or in my apartment. I didn't want anything around to tie me to the scam."

"Smart, very smart."

Trevor smiled and kept talking. "I can think like a criminal when I need to. I still haven't found the right detective in Philadelphia, but I'm working on it."

Brant White was a CIA creation. Trevor could hire every

detective in the Northeast, and they'd never find a real person behind the post-office box.

"In fact, I was preparing to go up there myself when Spicer phoned and told me to go to Washington to find out about Al Konyers. Then you guys showed up and, well, the rest is history." Trevor didn't think about a connection between Wes and Chap and the trip to Washington. He was thinking about leaving this cheap little office for the last time.

"Is there anyone else working on the scam outside?" Wes asked.

"Oh, no," Trevor said proudly. "I don't need any help. The fewer people involved, the easier the scam works."

At lunchtime Trevor was looking forward to a trip to Pete's and his first beer of the day, but Chap went out and brought back sandwiches and soft drinks. He also collected the mail from the Aladdin North mailbox. Trevor didn't need to go to the post office anymore. Chap would make sure that the CIA didn't miss a single letter. The six letters for Ricky were taken to the apartment across the street, opened, copied, and put back together.

After the day's mail was examined, a report was sent to Teddy Maynard's office. Sam Deville received it by 7 P.M.

◆

The telephone rang for the first time at five o'clock in the afternoon when Chap was fixing more coffee. Wes was still sitting at Trevor's desk, asking one question after another. Trevor was tired and desperately needed a beer.

"Answer it," Wes told Trevor.

"Hello," Trevor said weakly.

"Trevor, this is Joe Roy Spicer. What'd you find in Washington?"

"We're still working on it. It's going to be a difficult one, but we'll find him."

After a long pause, Spicer said, "Bring $5,000 in cash when you come tomorrow."

"Why do you—"

"Don't ask stupid questions, Trevor. Get the money and bring it. In twenties and fifties. You've done it before."

"All right."

Cash was against the rules at Trumble, but there was plenty of it around. It was smuggled in and hidden, and it was used to pay gambling debts and to buy things from the guards. Trevor was nervous about getting caught with cash, but he'd smuggled in $500 on two previous occasions.

He couldn't imagine what they wanted with $5,000.

◆

Chap and Wes announced that they were going to drive Trevor to Trumble the next day.

"I don't need a driver," Trevor explained. "I've made this trip a thousand times, and I always go alone."

Wes and Chap finally agreed, but they followed Trevor as he drove to the prison. A white van, with people Trevor would never see, drove behind the agents' rental car.

As he got closer to Trumble, Trevor started to worry a bit. Could he talk to Spicer and give him the letters as usual? Could he stay calm with a powerful listening device at the bottom of his briefcase? He felt guilty for a few seconds, but told himself that there was no honor among thieves. Anyway, he'd already sold his soul to Wes and Chap's client.

At the lawyers' room Trevor saw Spicer behind his newspaper. Guilt hit him, but he couldn't turn back now.

The guard checked Trevor's briefcase, and the CIA agents in the white van outside heard him say to Trevor, "It looks fine." The listening device was covered by a pile of papers. "I'll be outside."

They heard the door close, and suddenly there was silence. A very long silence. Nothing. Not a word between lawyer and client. They waited anxiously in the white van, but it was obvious that something had gone wrong.

As the guard stepped out of the small room, Trevor had quickly set the briefcase outside the door, on the floor, where it stayed during his meeting with Spicer.

"What'd you do that for?" Spicer asked.

"It's empty," Trevor said. "The guard and the camera can see that we have nothing to hide." He'd simply tell Wes and Chap that the guard took his briefcase, something that happened occasionally.

Spicer looked through the mail and found a thick envelope. "Is this the money?"

"Yeah, it's all there."

"So what happened in Washington?"

"Not much. It's a difficult case. We just need a little more time."

"What detective are you using?" asked Spicer.

"Some guy in Chevy Chase."

"Give me a name."

Trevor couldn't think of anything quickly. "I can't remember."

"Where'd you stay?"

"Why do you want to know?" asked Trevor. He needed time to think of something.

"What flight did you take?"

"I don't remember."

"You got back yesterday. Less than twenty-four hours ago, and you can't remember anything about your trip? Are you sure you went to Washington?" Spicer asked accusingly.

"Of course I went," said Trevor, but his voice broke a little because he was lying.

"You must think I'm stupid," Spicer said and leaned across the table. "I've got some bad news for you, Trevor. You're fired. We're removing your name as our lawyer and official visitor. When you leave today, you won't be able to come back, Trevor."

"Why?"

"Lying, drinking too much, lack of trust."

"What about the scam? Who'll run it on the outside?"

"We'll worry about that. Get up, walk out, it's been great."

"Sure," Trevor managed to say. He was shocked. It wasn't fair, but pride made him stand. He held out his hand and said, "Sorry it had to happen."

Spicer shook his hand unenthusiastically.

When they looked at each other for the last time, Trevor felt guilty. He quickly said, almost in a whisper, "Konyers is your man. Very rich. Very powerful. He knows about you."

Spicer jumped up like a cat. He stared into Trevor's eyes and whispered, "Is he watching you?"

Trevor shook his head and then opened the door. He picked up his briefcase and said goodbye to the guards, same as always but now for the last time. He ignored the white van and Wes and Chap in the car behind him as he drove toward Jacksonville.

◆

Their decision to fire Trevor had been reached after hours of discussion. Someone had found out about the scam. It probably happened because the lawyer was not careful enough. The only problem was that he could take their money, and they couldn't stop him. But they were happy to take that risk because they were expecting a big payday from Mr. Aaron Lake. To get to Lake, they felt that they had to get rid of Trevor.

Spicer hurried back to the library and told Beech and Yarber every word of his conversation with Trevor. Konyers was watching Trevor. He knew about the Brethren. Did that mean Lake knew about the Brethren? Why did Trevor whisper this and why did he leave his briefcase outside the door?

The judges asked questions, and then they made their plans.

Chapter 11   Trevor and Buster on the Move

Trevor was making coffee in his apartment when Wes and Chap arrived.

"What happened?" Wes asked. "Why couldn't we hear anything?"

"It was all routine. Sometimes the guard takes the briefcase and keeps it outside. He does it about once a month."

"And was the meeting just routine, too?"

"Yes, but Spicer didn't have any mail for me. That happens, too. I'll go back in two days and he'll have a pile of letters for me, and the guard won't touch the briefcase. You'll hear every word. Want some coffee?"

"No, thanks. We'd better go." They had reports to write, questions to ask.

"Look, you guys," Trevor said politely. "I can get dressed and showered by myself. Let's meet at the office at nine, OK?"

"Sure," one of them said, and they were gone. They had listening devices all over the office, the house, the car, even the briefcase now. They weren't worried about losing Trevor.

After they left, Trevor drank several cups of coffee, and then he began to follow his own plan. He knew that he was being watched all the time, so he had to be very careful.

He drove to a shopping mall about twenty kilometers away, near Orange Park. He ate a pizza, bought a cell phone and a pair of pants with lots of deep pockets. He went into the restroom and changed into the new pants. Then he stuffed his cash into the deep pockets.

At ten o'clock the mall closed and Trevor went to Pete's, where Wes and Chap would expect him to go. He ordered a beer and sat at a quiet table in the corner. When he had his second beer in front of him, he put his briefcase under the table and went to the men's restroom. He quickly climbed through the window and escaped into the night. He went toward the beach, trying to look like a man taking an innocent late evening walk.

After four or five kilometers, Trevor left the beach and walked into a cheap little hotel. He rang the bell on the desk and a thin young man of no more than twenty came out from the back and said, "Good evening. Need a room?"

"No, sir," Trevor said, as he slowly pulled out a roll of cash. "I need a little help. What's your name?"

"Sammy," the boy said nervously.

"All right, Sammy. Here's $1,000. It's yours if you'll drive me to Daytona Beach. It'll take you ninety minutes."

"It'll take me three hours because I have to drive back."

"But that's still $300 an hour. No one'll ever know you've been gone, and you'll have $1,000."

"I'll do it for $2,000."

In ninety-eight minutes Trevor was in Daytona Beach and Sammy was driving north again. At 1:20 A.M. Trevor had some coffee and toast in a little café, and at about two, a taxi dropped him off at the Daytona Beach International Airport. He found dozens of small private planes parked on one side of the airfield.

Several of the planes were for rent and Trevor began phoning the numbers he found posted outside a small office building. Finally, a pilot named Eddie agreed to get out of bed and fly Trevor to Nassau for his regular charge plus an extra $2,000. Trevor was standing outside the Nassau Trust Bank at nine o'clock the next morning.

Trevor pushed into Mr. Brayshears' office and demanded to be helped immediately. He had $900,000 in his private account from Mr. Al Konyers plus $68,000 from his business with the Brethren. With advice from Mr. Brayshears, Trevor moved all of his money to a new account in Bermuda. He planned to keep moving the money until he felt safe.

For one short moment, he thought about the money in the Brethren's account: just over $189,000. His name was on the account, too, and the money was his if he asked for it. They'd fired him. He tried to hate them, but he ended up feeling sorry for them. Three old men wasting their lives in prison.

A million was enough. Besides, he was in a hurry. He wouldn't be surprised if Wes and Chap suddenly burst into the bank with guns. He thanked Brayshears and ran from the building.

He headed for the Nassau International Airport and was in

the air with Eddie again before eleven o'clock. They landed on Eleuthera, an island Trevor had seen in a travel magazine. There were beaches, hotels, and lots of water sports. He paid Eddie in cash and took a taxi to an expensive hotel on the beach. He bought some new clothes and stopped looking over his shoulder. Surely even Mr. Konyers wasn't rich enough to have a secret army watching every corner of the Bahamas. Trevor was going to forget about the past and enjoy his new life.

◆

Wes and Chap had seen Trevor enter Pete's the night before. Then they sat in the parking lot and waited for him to come out at closing time, but he never appeared. The signals from the listening device in his briefcase told them that he was still inside the bar. They waited until 3 A.M. before they broke into Pete's and discovered that Trevor was not with his briefcase.

CIA agents went through everything in Trevor's office, car, and apartment. Not surprisingly, they didn't find any clues about where he'd gone. He'd just walked away, with the cash.

Eventually they found a banking official in Nassau who would cooperate with the CIA. He would only state that Trevor Carson had visited a bank in Nassau and had moved his money. He wouldn't give them any other details.

The United States customs office could tell the CIA that Trevor's passport had been checked as he entered Nassau that morning, and he hadn't left the Bahamas, at least not officially. His passport was now on a special list, and the government would know immediately if he tried to enter another country.

At Langley, York was with Teddy Maynard.

"He'll make a mistake," York said. "He'll use his passport somewhere, and we'll catch him."

Teddy was really angry, but he had to forget about the lawyer and worry about Aaron Lake.

"We paid a million dollars for a contact that lasted for one visit to Trumble. We have to have someone inside the prison."

"Kenny Sands'll be ready in forty-eight hours. He has eleven years with the CIA, age thirty-nine, very good results at every job. He'll arrive at Trumble just like any federal prisoner. His name for this job will be Wilson Argrow."

"Get him in there today. We need to know how much the three judges know about Al Konyers."

"We don't think they know anything. He's just another one of their pen pals. We stopped the lawyer from finding out his real name. He's off in the Bahamas, getting drunk with his money."

"I'll feel better when he's dead," Teddy said.

◆

A guard came for Finn Yarber, Hatlee Beech, and Joe Roy Spicer the next afternoon and led them to the main office of the prison. Emmitt Broon, the top official at Trumble, was waiting for them.

"The Jacksonville police tell me that your lawyer is missing. He hasn't been seen since last night at about ten o'clock."

Their faces didn't change, but each of the judges was thinking about their money.

"Why are you telling us?" Beech asked.

"If he contacts you, I want to know immediately."

They returned to the library, wondering if Aaron Lake had anything to do with this.

◆

Buster's escape was less complicated than a trip to the supermarket. The Brethren were in the sports area, watching for guards, but they didn't expect to see any.

Buster was working in the same area. When Spicer gave him the signal, Buster put his tools down, walked across the grass, and was gone. The three judges watched him go. No one would notice that a prisoner was missing until the end of the day. Then the guards would look for him for a few hours before informing the local police that a prisoner had walked away.

So Buster had most of the day to get as far away from Trumble as possible. He also had $2,000 in cash, given to him by Finn Yarber, a map that Beech had drawn, and an envelope addressed to Al Konyers in Chevy Chase, Maryland. He was going to mail the letter at the first post office he found.

Everything worked perfectly. In a few hours Buster took some clothes from a clothesline near a farmhouse and walked into a small, rural town, looking like a typical twenty-year-old.

He found the post office and dropped the Brethren's important letter into the box marked Out-of-Town. Then he caught a bus to Gainesville, where he bought, for $480, a ticket that would take him anywhere in the United States for sixty days. He headed west. He wanted to get lost in Mexico.

Chapter 12   Waiting for Aaron Lake

Over breakfast, the Brethren read the Jacksonville morning paper. They read that Aaron Lake had beaten Governor Tarry in Pennsylvania and Indiana. Tarry had announced that he was retiring from the race for the White House. Aaron Lake was now his party's official candidate. In November the contest would be between Lake and the Vice President for the highest office in the land. The Brethren were now Aaron Lake's strongest supporters. Run, Aaron, run.

The news of Buster's escape hadn't caused any excitement at Trumble. Good for him, the other prisoners were saying. He was a kid with a long sentence. Run, Buster, run.

The Brethren wouldn't be writing more letters; none would be brought in because they'd lost their outside contact. Their business now was to wait for Mr. Aaron Lake to contact them.

♦

Wilson Argrow arrived at Trumble in a green van. The officials there thought he was a real prisoner with a sixty-month sentence for taking money from the bank he worked for. He was thirty-nine years old, separated from his wife, college-educated, and his home address was in Coral Gables, Florida.

A guard showed Argrow around and ended with the library. The guard pointed to a corner and said, "That's the law library."

"Who uses it?" Argrow asked.

"Right now we have three judges who use it most of the time."

At the end of the tour Argrow thanked the guard, and about an hour later returned to the library. He went to the corner and opened the door to the law library.

Joe Roy Spicer looked up and saw a man he'd never seen before. "Looking for something?" he asked rather rudely.

Argrow recognized the face from his file. A Justice of the Peace caught selling local government contracts.

"I'm new," he said. "Can anybody use the law library?"

"I guess so," Spicer said. "You a lawyer?"

"No, a banker." Argrow excused himself and returned to his room.

Contact was made.

◆

Aaron Lake knew that he couldn't return to his all-night mailbox again. He had too many people with him night and day. He'd have to depend on someone else to help him get rid of the last memories of Ricky.

The young lady's name was Jayne Cordell. She earned $55,000 a year as one of his personal campaign assistants. She was always at his side, ready to do anything that he asked. She was totally, unquestioningly loyal to Aaron Lake.

At the right moment, he'd ask her to take his key and collect the mail from the box rented to Mr. Al Konyers. Then end the contract for the box, and leave no forwarding address. He'd explain that he'd had the box to receive secret information for a congressional report. She'd believe him because she wanted to believe him.

If he was lucky, there would be no letter from Ricky. The box would be forever closed.

He waited for the right moment. He waited too long.

◆

The Brethren's letter arrived in Al Konyers' mailbox in Chevy Chase three days after Buster dropped it off. A CIA agent found the letter on one of his routine checks of the box. The envelope was examined, then quickly taken to Langley.

The handwriting was familiar. Teddy Maynard knew the letter was serious trouble before he began reading.

Dear Al

In your last letter you tried to end our relationship. Sorry, it won't be that easy. I'm not Ricky, and you're not Al. I'm a prisoner in Trumble Federal Prison.

I know who you are, Mr. Lake. I know you're having a great year, and you have all that money pouring in.

I need money—that'll be easy for you—and I want out of prison, which may be complicated. But I'm sure you'll think of something. I'll be happy to remain silent if I get what I want. I'm willing to ruin you if I don't.

Find a way to contact me, and do it quickly.

I will not go away.

Sincerely, Joe Roy Spicer

Deville and York met with Teddy Maynard in his office. Argrow could kill the three judges with the right tools: pills, poison, or an accident. But there were problems with this solution. First, it was messy, and it'd be unusual if three friends died more or less at the same time. Second, what would happen if Trevor heard about the deaths? Maybe he knew more than they thought. Maybe he'd do something unexpected if he was scared.

Finally, the Brethren might still have a contact on the outside. If Argrow killed them, this fourth person could still cause trouble. Spicer and Yarber both had wives who might know something. The Lake letters were valuable. Someone else probably had copies of them. If the Brethren were killed, the letters might be taken to the newspapers, or even to the police.

"Maybe we should put the letter back in the box and let Aaron Lake find it for himself. Let him take care of this mess. He created it," said Deville.

"Actually, we created it," Teddy said, "and we'll deal with it."

They couldn't control what Lake might do. Somehow he'd gotten something in the mail to Ricky without their knowledge. And he'd been so stupid that the Brethren now knew who he was.

Teddy tried to keep his eye on the big picture. The "Lake mess" was a little problem compared with Natty Chenkov. He could get rid of Aaron Lake, but Lake was an important part of Teddy's plans for stopping the Russians. He'd wait, be patient, find a better way to deal with this mess.

The meeting was interrupted by an urgent message from Deville. Trevor Carson's passport had been checked in Bermuda. He was on a flight to San Juan, Puerto Rico that would land there in about fifty minutes.

"Have someone waiting for him," said Teddy.

Chapter 13   Follow the Money

Joe Roy Spicer was waiting for the Jacksonville paper the next morning, so he saw the story first, at the bottom of the front page.

Trevor Carson, a local lawyer who had been missing for a few days, had been found dead outside a hotel in San Juan, Puerto Rico, shot twice in the head last night, just after dark. According to the Puerto Rican officials, Trevor was a tourist who had been robbed. His wallet was missing, but someone at the scene gave the police his name.

Spicer rushed out and found Beech and Yarber in the cafeteria. They sat together in a corner, away from everyone else, picking at their food, talking in quiet voices.

"Who was he running away from?" wondered Yarber.

"Maybe Lake was after him," suggested Beech.

"He didn't know that it was Lake. He didn't have a clue. He told me that Konyers was the big one. He said Konyers knew about us, then he left the country the next day," said Spicer.

"Maybe he was scared. Maybe he took all the money he could get his hands on and left his troubles behind," said Yarber.

"Someone knew that Trevor was the outside contact for Ricky," said Spicer. "They put pressure on him and he ran. But Trevor didn't know that Lake was Konyers. He was running away from Konyers."

"What about us?" asked Beech. "Somebody knows that Joe Roy is Ricky, and that he has partners with him in prison."

"The question is, can these people get to us?" added Yarber.

"And," said Spicer, "did Trevor steal our money?"

Each of the judges needed time to think. Beech and Yarber went back to their rooms; Spicer went to the law library, where he found Mr. Argrow, the new prisoner, reading law books.

Argrow looked up and said, "Good morning."

Usually no one went into this part of the library without asking one of the Brethren first, but Argrow was new, so Joe Roy decided to be polite.

"Morning," said Spicer. "How are you doing?"

"OK, thanks. My roommate told me something interesting. He says that you and your friends do legal work."

"That depends on the case," Spicer said cautiously.

"I got sixty months for taking money from the bank I worked for in Miami and hiding it in the Bahamas. I've been in for four months, but I don't think I can last another fifty-six."

Money in the Bahamas made Spicer interested in Argrow's case.

"Are you guilty?"

"Sure. I dealt with millions every day. Lots of it was from drugs. I could move dirty money around quicker than any banker in Florida. I wanted some of it for myself and got caught. But I think the judge gave me a hard sentence. Five years is a long time."

Spicer was getting more and more interested.

"We can take a look at your case, but I can't promise anything."

"What will it cost?"

"How much do you have?" Spicer asked, just like a real lawyer.

"Not much. I had a nice fat account in the Bahamas, but I let it get away."

"So you can't pay anything?"

"Not much. Maybe $1,000 or so."

"You said you were good at moving dirty money around. Can you still do business in the Bahamas?"

"Sure. I still have some good friends in the Caribbean."

"Meet me here in an hour," said Spicer.

◆

When Argrow returned to the law library, the three judges were waiting for him.

"Mr. Spicer tells us you're an expert on moving dirty money around," Beech said.

"I was until I got caught," Argrow said. "I guess you have some."

"We have a small account, money that we've earned by doing work from here, but we don't know if the money is still in the account or not."

"What do you mean?" asked Argrow.

"We had a lawyer who took care of our business on the outside. He left town. We'd like to know if he took our money with him," explained Beech.

"That shouldn't be difficult. Which bank?"

"The Nassau Trust, in the Bahamas."

"You're lucky that you picked the Bahamas," said Argrow.

"Well, the lawyer actually picked it," Spicer said.

"Anyway, the system is pretty loose there. Secrets get told. The best place to hide money these days is Panama or Grand Cayman," said Argrow, as the banking expert.

"Here's the deal. You check our account, and we'll look at your case for free," said Beech. "Can you do it?"

"I can try. No guarantees," said Argrow. "Give me the name and the account number and I'll make a few phone calls."

"You can't use the phones here," said Spicer. "They aren't safe."

"This is a telephone, gentlemen," said Argrow, as he took a very small instrument from his pocket.

The Brethren stared at the thing in Argrow's hand.

"Who pays the bill?" asked Beech.

"I have a brother in Boca Raton. He gave me the phone and the service, so now I'll start work. Is there a private room around here?"

The judges showed him into their conference room and shut the door. They sat outside and watched as Argrow made several telephone calls. They thought he was talking to bankers in Nassau, but he was really talking to CIA agents in the white van parked a couple of kilometers from the prison.

After an hour, Argrow came out of the room and said he was making progress. "I need to wait an hour, then make a few more calls. I'll be back after lunch."

With Argrow gone, the judges returned to their other concerns. It had been six days since Buster had left with their letter. No word from Buster meant he'd walked away without problems, mailed the note to Mr. Konyers, and was now somewhere far away. Aaron Lake should have the letter and be very worried by now.

They intended to give Lake a week, and then contact him again if they hadn't heard from him—they might even ask Argrow if they could use his secret phone. This was their big chance to make a lot of money and, more importantly, to get out of prison. But they had to work fast. Aaron Lake was only valuable to them if he was an important man. If he lost the election in November, he'd be forgotten like all losers.

◆

Following Mr. Lake's exact instructions, Jayne Cordell drove alone to Chevy Chase and parked in front of Mailbox America. She used Mr. Lake's key and emptied the box of eight pieces of mail—all advertisements. Then she informed the woman behind the desk that she was closing the account for her employer, and handed in the key.

Jayne returned to the campaign offices and had a quick word with Aaron Lake. He was happy to see that there were no personal letters. Nothing from Ricky.

After Jayne left his office, Lake smiled and almost laughed. Then, with his typical energy, he jumped up from his chair, put on his jacket, and began another day of meetings and speeches.

Oh what a lucky man!

◆

In the afternoon, Argrow was back in the conference room making more phone calls and pretending to sort out the Brethren's bank account. He finally came out after two hours.

"Good news, gentlemen, you still have just over $190,000 in your account."

The judges knew that he was telling the truth because he got the amount right. They smiled and relaxed a bit.

"Your lawyer obviously didn't take your cash," said Argrow, "but I suggest you move it to Panama. Your money's not safe in the Bahamas. Look how easily I found someone to give me information about your account, and besides, you should put that money to work. You could be earning 15 to 20 percent a year. You're not going to be using it any time soon anyway."

That's what you think, Mr. Argrow, they thought.

"Can you move it for us?" asked Spicer.

"Of course I can, for a price. I get 10 percent for moving it."

"That's expensive, isn't it?"

"It's common in the banking business. That's my price. Take it or leave it."

It was only $19,000, and besides, they were looking forward to a very big payday from Lake.

"It's a deal," Spicer said as he looked at his partners. If they got the serious money they expected from Lake, they'd need a safe place to hide it, and maybe someone to help them.

"Plus you look at my case," said Argrow.

"We'll look into it, but we can't promise anything."

"OK," said Argrow, and then he retired to the conference room and pretended to work again.

After an hour, he came out and said, "I think I can finish it tomorrow, but I'll need a statement with your signatures, saying that you are the owners of the account."

"Who will see the statement?" asked Beech.

"Only the bank in the Bahamas. They're getting a copy of Mr. Carson's death certificate, and now they have to deal with the three of you."

"How will we get the statement to the Bahamas? Trevor used to carry our mail out for us," said Yarber.

"Do the guards inspect the mail?"

"They take a quick look, but they can't open it."

"Just a second," said Argrow, and then he opened his phone again. "Hello. Wilson Argrow here. Is Jack in? Tell him it's important." He waited.

"Who in the world is Jack?" asked Spicer.

"My brother in Boca Raton," Argrow said. "He's also my lawyer, and he's bringing all of the papers from my case to me tomorrow." Then, into the phone, he said, "Jack, come tomorrow at around ten. I'll have some mail going out. See you then."

A banker with a phone and with a brother who was a lawyer. He was beginning to look like a pretty good partner.

"Can we trust your brother?" asked Spicer.

"With your life," Argrow said. He was walking to the door. "I'll see you guys later. I need some fresh air."

◆

The second Argrow brother was really Roger Lyter, a CIA agent for thirteen years with a law degree from Texas. He met Kenny Sands, who was Wilson Argrow, on his first visit to Trumble. He arrived carrying a box full of papers.

"What's in there?" the guard asked.

"It's my client's court records," answered Jack Argrow.

"Just paperwork," added Wilson Argrow.

The guard took a quick look and then stepped out of the room.

Wilson handed a paper to Jack, and said, "This is the statement for the bank in Nassau. We need to put $171,000 in a new bank account in Panama so that I have the papers to show these guys."

The Nassau Trust Bank would never be contacted. No bank would close an account with no more than the kind of statement that the Brethren had signed. The money going to Panama was new money.

"The bosses at Langley are getting anxious," said Jack.

"I'm ahead of schedule," reported Wilson.

Chapter 14   The Final Solution

A CIA agent pushed Teddy Maynard's wheelchair into the back of a special van. He was tired: tired of his work, tired of the battle, tired of getting through another day, then another. Fight for six more months, he kept telling himself, then let someone else worry about saving the world. He'd go quietly to his farm in West Virginia, watch the leaves fall into the lake, and wait for the end. He was so tired of the pain.

Teddy didn't like having meetings with the President. The last time they'd seen each other was nine months earlier when Teddy was in the hospital and the President needed advice on handling a problem with the Chinese. And, even more, Teddy hated asking the President for a favor. He liked to be asked for favors, not do the asking. This president owed Teddy several favors, but Teddy still didn't enjoy doing the asking.

The CIA chief was shown into a small room next to the President's personal office. A busy secretary explained without apologizing that the President was in another meeting. Teddy smiled and knew he was being kept waiting on purpose. The President wanted to show him who was in charge.

The President finally arrived in a rush, and the two men went into the office for a simple lunch of salad and grilled chicken. They talked about recent political situations in France and North Korea. The President asked about Teddy's health.

"I'll probably leave the job when you do," Teddy explained.

This pleased the President for some reason, and then he began a rather long discussion of the presidential campaign. He praised his Vice President and criticized Aaron Lake because of his position on defense.

"How do you see the race?" the President finally asked.

"I honestly don't care," Teddy lied. "As I told you, I'm leaving Washington when you do, Mr. President. I'm tired, sir." They were wasting time, and Teddy wanted to be back at Langley. "I'm here for a favor," he said slowly.

"Yes, I know. What can I do for you?" The President was chewing and smiling, enjoying the rare moment when Teddy had to ask for something.

"I'd like pardons for three federal prisoners."

"Spies?" the President asked. Pardons were usually a simple matter unless foreign spies were involved.

"No. Judges. They're serving time together in a federal prison."

Teddy explained why the three judges were in prison. The President listened and asked questions. He didn't want to make things easy for Teddy.

"Do you know these men?" the President asked.

"No. But I know their friends," Teddy said.

The President knew that this was a lie, and he knew that he wasn't going to get the whole story from Teddy.

"Will this do any damage to me or to the Vice President?"

"No, sir. I don't think the public will even notice. And, if it will make things easier, these gentlemen will agree to leave the country for at least two years."

"Why?"

"If they went home, people might want to know why they got out early. This can be kept very quiet," explained Teddy. "There's nothing to worry about, Mr. President. I'm asking for a small favor. With a little luck, this will not be reported anywhere."

Soon the two men shook hands. The deal was done.

◆

Wilson Argrow found Joe Roy Spicer in the sports area.

"Mr. Spicer, we need to have a meeting," Argrow said. "I have the papers to show that your money is now in Panama."

"That's good news. Anything else?"

"My brother has talked to Aaron Lake."

Spicer stopped and looked at Argrow. "We'll meet you in the law library in half an hour."

Argrow was ten minutes late, but he began the meeting as soon as he arrived.

"I only know what my brother has told me," he began. "Yesterday some people who work for Aaron Lake contacted him. They knew that I was here. They made promises, and they made him swear to keep things secret." Then he laid a copy of their last letter to Al Konyers on the table.

"I guess you know everything, don't you?" Spicer asked.

"I know that you're running a scam. You advertise in gay magazines, you start pen–pal relationships with older men, and you then blackmail them for money. And Mr. Lake made the mistake of answering one of your advertisements."

"That's about all of it," Spicer said.

"So what's your job in this?" asked Beech.

"I'm just the messenger, but if things work out the way Mr. Lake wants, then I get out of here early. That's what my brother asked for. Now the question is, what do you guys want to bury this story forever?"

"You've got the letter. We want some money and we want out of this place."

"How much money?"

"Two million dollars each. We read the papers. We know Mr. Lake has more money than he can spend right now. Six million is nothing to him," Spicer said.

"I can't make the deal—like I said, I'm just the messenger, like Trevor was."

They froze when they heard the name of their dead lawyer. They wondered if this was a warning to them. They were excited about getting their freedom, but they wondered how safe they'd be.

They'd always know Lake's secret.

"We want out of this place now, and we want our money put in a bank account in London," Beech said. Then he added, "It has to be clean. We don't want to be running for the rest of our lives. We don't want to be looking over our shoulders. If we get what we want, Mr. Lake won't have anything to worry about. But if anything happens to us, his story will be told."

"We have an outside contact," Yarber said. "If something happens to any of us, he'll tell everything."

"I'll see my brother at nine in the morning," Argrow said. "Let's meet here at ten. Maybe he'll know something then."

Argrow left the three judges deep in thought, counting their money but afraid to start spending it. The CIA agent found a quiet spot and reported to Deville. Teddy Maynard knew what was going on at Trumble less than an hour later.

◆

The Brethren met at breakfast the next morning. None of them had slept the night before. How many more days would they eat prison food, wear prison clothes, and dream of the future?

"Argrow's making me nervous," Yarber said.

"Why's that?"

"He turns up here from nowhere, and suddenly he's our best friend. He does a magic trick with our money, and now he's Aaron Lake's messenger. Remember, somebody was reading our mail, and it wasn't Lake."

"Yeah, and it's very convenient that he has a brother that someone found," Beech said. "There's somebody else out there."

"Do we really care?" asked Spicer. "If somebody can get us out of here, I'm going to be very grateful."

"But don't forget what happened to Trevor," said Yarber.

"Aaron Lake wouldn't kill us. It'd be too risky," said Spicer.

"No, he wouldn't, but the mystery man would. The guy who killed Trevor is the same guy who read our mail."

"You can't be sure," said Spicer, but he was nervous, too.

They were still talking when Argrow found them together in the law library.

"I just met with my brother," he said. "Lake will pay the money." Argrow looked at his watch and then checked the door. "There are some people from Washington here to meet with you."

He pulled some papers from his pocket and placed a single sheet in front of each man. "These are copies of your presidential pardons, signed yesterday."

"We've been pardoned?" Yarber finally managed to ask in a dry voice.

"Yes. By the President of the United States. You'll get the news officially in a few minutes. Act surprised."

"That should be easy," said Yarber.

"You'll be out of here in an hour. A van will take you to Jacksonville to a hotel where my brother will meet you. He'll have information about your money waiting in London. You'll give him all of the files you have on Al Konyers and Aaron Lake. Everything. Understood?"

They agreed. For $2 million each, they could have it all.

"You will agree to leave the country immediately, and not to return for at least two years. My brother has new names, passports, and money for you."

A guard knocked on the door. It was time to meet the men from Washington.

"Do we have a deal, gentlemen?" asked Argrow.

Spicer wasn't sure about leaving the country. He wanted to go home. Yarber turned and looked at him. "Are you crazy? A complete pardon, a million dollars a year for two years."

They shook hands with Argrow and then followed the guards to the main office. There was a short ceremony during which they were presented with their official pardons like prizes for service to their country.

The government official said, "The President has looked at your cases, and feels that you have served enough time. He believes strongly that you have more to offer your country by becoming useful, productive citizens again."

The Brethren stared at him. He obviously knew nothing about their scam or their new names or their $2 million each. The judges had no idea who was helping them, but they were not going to ask any questions now.

They hurried back to their rooms and packed up the few things they owned. They wanted to be out of Trumble before the dream ended, or before the President changed his mind.

Chapter 15   The Brethren's Bright Future

At 11:15, the Brethren walked through the front door of the main building and got into a van driven by Wes and Chap. Spicer wanted a beer and he wanted a woman, preferably his wife. Hatlee Beech began to cry, not loud, but with his eyes tightly closed. Yarber held on to his pardon and stared out the window.

They arrived at an expensive hotel in Jacksonville and were led to a room for a meeting with Jack Argrow.

"Have a seat," Argrow said. "How's my brother?"

"He's doing well," Beech said. "We saw him this morning."

"I want him out of prison," Argrow said. "Look, I don't know what you've done. I'm here because I have a deal with Aaron Lake. I've never met Mr. Lake, but if I do this for him, he'll do a couple of favors for me. I don't know everything, you understand?" He talked quickly and couldn't sit still.

Two hidden cameras in the room allowed Teddy and York to watch the meeting. It was interesting to see the three judges for the first time. Their scam had caught Aaron Lake, and now they'd get their money and their freedom.

"Your money is in a large bank in London called City Trust. Here are the documents. We need to take your photographs so we can finish your passports. When do you want to leave Jacksonville?"

"I want to go to London today," Yarber said. "Spicer and Beech will meet me there tomorrow if all goes well." The three men had obviously discussed their plans.

"Things will go well. I guarantee it," said Argrow. "Now, go next door and have your pictures taken. Then go out to lunch and come back at about four o'clock. Here's $5,000 each for spending money. I'll have your passports, credit cards, and your tickets waiting for you. And, can you leave your file on Aaron Lake before you go?"

The three men went to the hotel shop and bought new clothes, and then they had their pictures taken. They left the hotel on foot, with no guards and no rules. The world was pretty again. The sky was clear. Hope filled the air. They smiled and laughed at almost everything. They were ready for some fun.

They sat in an outdoor café and ate steak and drank beer. They watched people walk past and thought about the future. After lunch it was time to see Jack Argrow again and finish the deal.

Yarber left two hours later, traveling as Mr. William McCoy of San Jose, California. He flew to Atlanta and then on to London that evening. All first class. He was afraid to sleep because he was afraid to wake up and find himself back in Trumble.

Spicer found a pay phone near the hotel and called his wife.

"Darling, it's me. I'm out of prison. I'm at a hotel in Jacksonville, Florida. They let me out this morning," Joe Roy said excitedly.

"But why——?"

"Don't ask any questions. I'll explain everything later. I'm leaving for London tomorrow. Get a passport and join me there."

"England? I can't go to England. Why don't you come home?"

"I can't. It's part of the deal. I'll be away for two years."

"Joe Roy, did you escape? Are you in more trouble?"

"No. Everything's fine. Think about getting a passport."

♦

Mr. William McCoy arrived in London the next morning and went directly to the main City Trust offices. They made him wait for an hour, but he didn't mind. He'd learned how to be patient. Finally he talked to someone and moved all of the money from London to Switzerland.

That afternoon Beech and Spicer, as James Nunley and Harvey Moss, flew across the Atlantic. Yarber as Mr. McCoy met them at Heathrow Airport. He told them the wonderful news that the money had come and gone, and surprised them with the plan of flying immediately to Rome.

♦

Buster traveled by bus to San Diego. He wanted to be near the ocean again. Soon he was working for a man who owned several expensive fishing boats in Los Cabos, Mexico. The customers were rich Americans who spent more time drinking than fishing. He made plenty of money from tips and lived comfortably in a small hotel. Los Cabos quickly became his home.

◆

Aaron Lake arrived at Langley for lunch with the CIA director. In three days Lake's party would introduce him as their official presidential candidate. It'd be a happy occasion. Everything had gone according to Teddy's plan.

After greeting each other, Teddy said quite weakly, "This election belongs to you, Mr. Lake."

"I feel good about it, but it'll still be a fight."

"Sometimes the Vice President will be ahead in the polls, but in the middle of October there will be a political situation that will frighten the whole world. And you, Mr. Lake, will be seen as the only man who can take care of it."

"A war?" asked Lake.

"I hope not, but the situation will bring us close to a war, and Natty Chenkov will be blamed for it. Things will look very dangerous. The American public will vote for you because you have promised to handle these situations. Keep sending out your message, Mr. Lake."

"I will," said Lake seriously.

"Good," Teddy said, and closed his eyes for a moment. "Now, on a different topic. You need a partner, Mr. Lake, a First Lady, someone to make the White House a home for you. A young, pretty woman who will have children for you. I like this Jayne Cordell. She's thirty-eight, intelligent, and loyal. She'd make a fine wife for you."

"Are you crazy?" Lake asked. He was completely shocked by this suggestion.

"We know about Ricky," Teddy said coolly, with his eyes on Lake. Then he handed the candidate his last note to Ricky.

Dear Ricky

I think it's best if we stop writing letters to each other. I wish you well with your future.

Sincerely, Al

82

Lake almost said that he could explain things, but he decided to say nothing. His head was spinning. How much did they know? How did they get his mail?

Teddy let him suffer in silence. There was no hurry.

Then Lake started thinking like a politician again. He knew who was really in charge of his campaign. He swallowed and said, "I actually like her."

"Of course you do. She's perfect for the job. Hold hands with her for the TV cameras. Announce your wedding plans a week before the election. A big Christmas wedding."

"I like that," agreed Lake.

"Then have a baby as soon as possible. It will be nice to see young children in the White House again."

Lake smiled, but then looked worried again. He asked, "Will anyone ever know about Ricky?"

"No. He'll never write another letter, Mr. Lake. And you'll be so busy with your young children and with running the country that you won't have time to think about people like Ricky."

"Ricky who?"

"Good man, Lake."

"I'm very sorry, sir. It won't happen again."

"Forget about it. But no more surprises."

"No, sir."

◆

By late November, the Brethren had settled in Monte Carlo and were enjoying its beauty and the warm weather. They lived in the same small but handsome hotel, and they usually had breakfast together twice a week. They had different interests, but each of them knew where the others were at all times.

Finn Yarber was sitting at an outdoor café, enjoying a cup of good coffee, when he saw a familiar face. He tried to remember why he knew the face. The man walked over and sat at Yarber's table and said, "Hello, Finn. Remember me?"

Yarber looked at the face and drank his coffee calmly.

"Wilson Argrow, from prison," the man said, and Yarber put down his cup before he dropped it. "I just wanted to let you know that we're always around—if you need us."

Yarber laughed. "That doesn't seem likely." Still, he was surprised that Argrow knew where they were.

"Exciting news about Aaron Lake—now President Lake," said Argrow. "But maybe you don't read the newspapers. Maybe you read magazines like this one." He handed it to Yarber and showed him a page of advertisements. One of them was circled in red:

Single, white male in 20s looking for kind and discreet gentleman in 40s or 50s to exchange letters with.

"These advertisements all look the same to me," Yarber said. He closed the magazine and put it on the table.

"The post-office box is here in Monte Carlo."

"Look," said Yarber, "I don't know who you work for, but we haven't broken any laws. So get lost."

"Sure, Mr. Yarber, but $2 million isn't enough?"

Yarber drank his coffee and said, "You have to keep busy."

"I'll see you around," Argrow said, then jumped to his feet and left as quickly as he'd appeared.

Yarber finished his coffee and watched the street for a few minutes. Then he left to find his two friends.

ACTIVITIES

Chapters 1–3

Before you read

1 Read the introduction to the book. Who are "the Brethren"?
2 Find the words in *italics* in your dictionary. They are all used in Chapters 1 and 2. Match each word with a clue (a–l).

brethren   campaign   candidate   case   charge   expert
federal   gamble   military   robe   sentence   urinate

   a worn by judges, church ministers, college graduates
   b ask him or her if you're in doubt
   c army, navy, air force
   d a reason to go to horse races, card games, sporting events
   e time in jail to pay for a crime
   f murder, theft, selling drugs, for example
   g vote for one of these on election day
   h a reason for needing a toilet
   i a formal word for members of a profession ("brothers")
   j work that comes before an election
   k bigger than state or local
   l presented formally in a court; heard by a judge and jury

3 Find the words in *italics* (from Chapter 3) in your dictionary. Answer the questions.

   a Can you name three different kinds of *account*?
   b How are guilt and shame important parts of *blackmail*?
   c What kind of professional people should be *discreet*?
   d Can you name a *gay* character in a movie or TV show?
   e Does a *pen pal* usually live near you or far away?
   f Is a *scam* a legal or illegal way to make money?

After you read

4 Make a list of the facts you know about the three Brethren. Is it probable that Beech, Spicer, and Yarber would have been friends if they had met outside prison? Why (not)?
5 Why does Teddy Maynard think Aaron Lake is the best man to become the next President of the United States?

Chapters 4–6

Before you read

6 Grisham begins two separate stories in Chapters 1–3. What are they? How do you think these two stories will come together?

7 Check the meaning of these words in your dictionary. Then read the clues and complete the word puzzle.

agent   briefcase   client   device   embassy   senator   terrorist Vice President

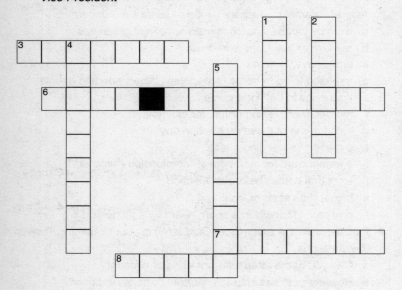

Across

3 A government's main building in a foreign country

6 The number two person in the American government

7 An elected official; there are two from each US state

8 A spy is one type

Down

1 An instrument or tool

2 A customer who pays for a professional service

4 It has a handle and carries books, pens, papers

5 Violence is her or her weapon

After you read

8 Work with a partner. Discuss the role of each of these people, events, and organizations in the development of the story.
  a Ricky
  b Trevor Carson
  c the Trilling factory
  d Senator Britt
  e Lufkin
  f Mr. Brayshears
  g Ms. Topolski
  h the Cairo bombing
  i Sam Deville

9 Match the people with their dreams. Then explain why these dreams are important to these men.
Trevor Carson   Aaron Lake   Quince Garbe   Teddy Maynard
The Brethren
  a A future outside Trumble
  b His father's death
  c An America safe from war
  d $1 million
  e A private life in the White House

10 Discuss these questions.
  a Why does Grisham mix the two big stories together in Chapters 4–6?
  b How do post-office box 455 in Maryland and box 44683 in Florida bring the two stories together?

Chapters 7–9

Before you read

11 Why is Teddy Maynard worried at this point in the story?

12 Look up *debate* and *poll* in your dictionary. Complete each sentence with one of these words.
  a A recent ..... claims that 60 percent of Americans go to church regularly.
  b Our teacher asked us to prepare talks for a ..... about gun control.

After you read

13 Are these statements true or false? Explain your answers with information from the story.

a The President is proud of his action against the city of Talah.
b After his third letter, the Brethren lose interest in Al Konyers.
c Natty Chenkov is becoming more dangerous to the US.
d Quince Garbe enjoys the visit from Chap and Wes.
e Brant White is a CIA agent.
f Lake believes that his letters to and from Ricky are his secret.
g The Brethren want to help Buster.
h Aaron Lake is the clear winner in his debate with Tarry.
i Aaron Lake enjoys a relaxing flight from Pittsburgh to St. Louis.
j The three letters from Al Konyers that arrive after April 18 are very exciting for the Brethren.

Chapters 10–12

Before you read

14 Discuss why the Brethren are feeling optimistic.

After you read

15 How are these people, things, and places important in Chapters 10–12?

a	Chap and Wes	f	Eddie
b	$1 million	g	Kenny Sands
c	$5,000	h	Buster
d	Trevor's briefcase	i	Jayne Cordell
e	Sammy	j	San Juan, Puerto Rico

Chapters 13–15

Before you read

16 What do you expect will happen to Trevor Carson when he arrives in Puerto Rico?

17 Find *favor* and *pardon* in your dictionary. Complete each sentence with the correct form of one of the two words.
    a "..... me. I didn't mean to be rude."
    b "Mom, can you do a ..... for me?"
    c The game was unfair because the judge ..... the competitor from his own country.

d With his . . . . . from the governor in his hand, the bank robber left prison after only two years.

After you read

18 Secrets and lies are important to the story.

    a What secret does Trevor keep from the Brethren?

    b What secret do "Wilson Argrow" and "Jack Argrow" keep from the Brethren?

    c What secret does Aaron Lake keep from Jayne Cordell?

    d What secrets does Teddy Maynard keep from the President?

    e What secret does the CIA keep from the officials at Trumble?

    f What secret does Joe Roy Spicer keep from his wife?

Writing

19 You are Mrs. Spicer. Write a letter to Joe Roy explaining why you are not going to join him in Monte Carlo.

20 Choose three characters from the story and discuss the importance of money to their behavior.

21 Write a short, positive report about Trevor Carson's life and death for his hometown newspaper in Pennsylvania.

22 You are Teddy Maynard. Choose three important days in your life and write about them in your private diary.

23 Write a telephone conversation between Jayne Cordell and her mother. Aaron Lake has just asked Jayne to marry him.

24 Grisham describes *The Brethren* as "probably the funniest" book he has written. Explain why you think this is/is not a funny book.

Answers for the Activities in this book are published in our free resource packs for teachers, the Penguin Readers Factsheets, or available on a separate sheet. Please write to your local Pearson Education office or to: Marketing Department, Penguin Longman Publishing, 5 Bentinck Street, London W1M 5RN.

BESTSELLING
PENGUIN READERS

AT LEVEL 5

The Body

The Firm

Four Weddings and a Funeral

The Great Gatsby

Jane Eyre

The Pelican Brief

The Prisoner of Zenda

Rebecca

Tales from Shakespeare

Taste and Other Tales

A Time to Kill

Wuthering Heights